SO-ARB-544

1.95

YOUR HELP IS AT HAND

By Mary L. Kupferle

Unity Books
Unity Village, MO 64065

Cover photo by Walt Mathison

Book designed by Linda Gates

CONTENTS

Lift Up Your Eyes

"I lift up my eyes to the hills. From whence does my help come? My help comes from the Lord, who made heaven and earth." — Ps. 121:1-2

There is never a time when you are without help! The loving Father's help is always at hand! When you feel your distress is more than you can bear, lift up your eyes to His presence and power through knowing: *My help is at hand! God, my Father, is always at hand!*

The vast, unlimited power of God—wisdom and light, peace and calm, life and strength, order and harmony, protection and deliverance—is all-present, ever-available, always where you are! God is the source of every miracle. God is the giver of every gift of supply, love, well-being, faith, courage, and inspiration. God, creator of your being, originator and sustainer of everything good and all you can ever deeply desire, is at hand!

Take a few minutes to become quiet, to go apart for awhile and listen within, then, speak to yourself about the following words and remember the Father's love for you, His child:

God's help is at hand. God, my Father, my

everlasting help, is at hand. God's help is mine now, and God is at work, doing whatever needs to be done. God's wisdom is lighting up my mind. God's power is strengthening my body. God's peace is calming my soul. My Father is at hand doing everything needful, good, and productive now!

There is no obstruction, no delay, nothing to hinder God's presence and power. God is my creator, my sustainer of healing life and peace ever lifting and supporting me. There is nothing in life I cannot do, face, surmount, overcome, or attain, for God is my help in every need. God is at hand, and I can let go and give thanks, for God is the kingdom, the power, and the glory, forever!

Lift up your eyes, the "eyes" of your mind and heart, to these words daily. Set an appointed time to reread them, to encourage your faith to return to them again and again. Establish them so strongly within that they become a solid foundation for all you say and do. Refuse to give credence to the slightest whisper of discouragement, impatience, or disbelief. Look away from any appearance that is negative by lifting up your eyes, your attention, to the presence of God.

Practice affirming your faith. Exercise the highest decrees of wholeness and well-being you can envision. Apply yourself to following the Master's teaching to keep your eye single, to serve only one Presence and one Power— God and good. Return again and again to the relationship of Creator and created as taught by Jesus Christ. Think about your own personal connection with the Father. Repeatedly remember your Father is at hand. Give your life's circumstances into God's care and keeping, knowing that God is doing all that is good, all that needs to be done, moment by moment.

Fortify your recognition of yourself as God's child, and strengthen this awareness by using words that express the closest relationship you can imagine having with the Father. This was the way of the One who quietly and powerfully taught the value of constant communion with God. Jesus talked with God clearly, simply, daily, directly, urging His followers to do the same.

Awareness of oneness with the Father is attainable for you, or the Master of such awareness would never have so insistently urged it. He wanted to help His listeners, to help you today to understand that your Father is at hand, ready to bless, prosper, heal, love, and provide everything helpful for His created. Jesus Christ wants you to know that the more often you seek that Presence—call upon it, depend upon it—the stronger the connection will become consciously, and the more at home you will feel in your communication with the author of your being.

The help you seek comes in many ways, for as God is infinite so is God's help for you infinite in its channeling and provision of supply and support of good. One person, feeling very much alone, needing reassurance and guidance during a difficult relationship challenge, was led to the local library for something uplifting to read. A book suddenly dropped from a shelf above where he stood. When he picked it up and replaced it, it dropped again. This time, as he stooped to retrieve it, the pages opening before him caught his eye. The words were like a flame of light, clear and direct, reassurance that God was at hand, with him in every detail of his life, guiding his way. God's help was at hand!

Another person, in need of healing, began listening to a tape recording that had been awaiting her attention and time of quiet. She reported, "I began listening to the tape and following its instructions for the blessing of the faculty of hearing. After a while I took off my wristwatch and held it over each ear in turn, and I could hear the ticking of my tiny wristwatch. For years, I had needed to ask my niece if it was going! Thank God for the help of the tape bringing me into a perfect healing of my ears!" God's help was at hand!

A retired businessman reported the help he needed was at hand as he read the Unity book *God Will See You Through*. With this encouragement and way of prayer, he was led into a successful experience in forming a new corporation. He found that he had a new feeling of wholeness and well-being within himself. He became more serene and peaceful, with mental and emotional calm. He said that help of every kind was at hand for him.

Help for healing, guidance, peace, upliftment, supply of every nature comes in manifold ways, sometimes unusual ways; many times help comes in quiet turns of thought or circumstances. You need place no limit upon how your help will come. You can, in all confidence, let go any human reasoning about how it will appear. Fasten your attention with quiet determination upon the idea: *God is at hand. His help is here, now.*

Lift up your vision of mind and heart often to this truth, knowing again and again that God is present, with you and within you, bringing to your opening awareness the answers you are ready to hear, the solutions you are ready to accept.

During a time when I personally needed to remember this, I began to affirm diligently: *God's help is at hand. My Father is doing His good work in and through and for me now.* I found that some of the most satisfying results of prayer quickly appeared not only for me, but also for others who had asked for spiritual support. Healings of illnesses, of inability to forgive, of grief and loss, of misunderstandings and disappointments, were reported as coming through in many different ways.

Yes, God is at hand! God's love is at hand! How good it is to know this, and then to trust God to do through you whatever needs to be done. Be assured, God's presence is here, on the spot. God's guidance is constant.

One friend wrote, "This idea has helped me to release extreme anxiety and concern regarding a friend who had been in agonizing pain for months. I held to your suggestion, knowing that God is at hand now. God is my help in every need. God is doing all that needs to be done. I refused to reason any longer about why the difficulty occurred, what the cause might be, how the help would come. Instead I constantly affirmed, in the face of every recurring doubt: *Your Father, your helper, your help is at hand. God is doing the work now.* Within a few days a total change was evident, with complete healing made visible. Thank God!

As you quietly listen in this moment, let go all but the thought, "My Father is at hand." His presence will be revealed in just the right way to ease your heart, revitalize your faith, and satisfy your deepest needs and longings. As you remember and recognize this reality, you will open up to a closer, richer communion with God's presence and power. You will feel freer to speak with God of your needs, hear more clearly God's guidance, be more confident in affirming your faith. You will understand that God honors your integrity in prayer—however faltering or uncertain it may be—as well as your desire to feel at one with Him. As a result, the right solutions and answers to every problem or test in life will be made known to you!

Give thanks that the work needing to be done in your life or another's is being done now by the One who knows best how to do it. Join the Psalmist in knowing, "The Lord is my strength and my shield; in him my heart trusts; so I am helped, and my heart exults, and with my song I give thanks to him" (Ps. 28:7).

Remember always that you are the offspring of God, the chosen channel and receiving vessel, the one through whom it is His delight to live and move and have being. You are the place God has selected to bring Himself into visibility right here on earth. His desire and intent is to shine through your mind as light and wisdom, through your heart as faith and love and compassion, through your body temple as strength and wholeness and well-being.

Lift up your eyes to the high vision that sees God's presence in action right where you are. Meditate upon this truth with thanksgiving. You, created in God's likeness, are substance of His substance, containing every potential of God. You are God's image. You are your Father's child, and His help is always at hand.

Yes, not only is your help always at hand, but it is ever within you, whoever and whatever you are. The more often you lift up your eyes to the hills of this reality, beholding your relationship with God, the more freely are you a channel through which God can flow, live, love, and bless. This is God's joy, to know that you know He is at hand. Accept your heritage, your Father's help now. God is at hand!

Your Healing Is at Hand

"Blessed is the man . . . [whose] delight is in the law of the Lord, and on his law he meditates day and night. He is like a tree planted by streams of water, that yields its fruit in its season, and its leaf does not wither. In all that he does, he prospers." — Ps. 1:1-3

The upliftment, strength, and courage you seek are at hand. Your sufficiency of everything needed for blessing of mind, body, or affairs is at hand. Regardless of where you are physically or how far you seem emotionally from the peace you desire, your good—your healing, your well-being, your fulfillment—is at hand.

Your healing is at hand. Healing of fears and anxieties, tensions and emotional upsets, is at hand. Release and freedom from concerns over any traumatic happenings or feelings of insecurity or defeat are at hand. Right where you are this moment, you are in the presence of the answers and solutions you have sought. Your good is tangible, touchable, and available to you now. Your good is at hand!

As you take a few moments to look about

you, remind yourself: *My healing is right here. It is in the air I breathe, the surroundings I see. It fills this space, and it lives within my heart. It is in the light of day and in the darkness of night. It is in the clouds and in the sunshine. It is in the cells and atoms of this body temple. It is in the movement of my mind and in the activity about me. My healing is at hand, and I accept it with praise and thanksgiving.*

Let the idea of healing penetrate every thought about yourself and all that appears to be occurring in your life. Acquaint yourself with the reality that healing is everywhere present, always. Practice faithfully seeing health with your mind's eye, in everything that comes across your path, reminding yourself that healing is here now, in this moment and circumstance, in this experience of life.

Keep turning your attention to the thoughts of healing of body, healing of feelings, healing of events, healing of conditions. Saturate your thinking with contemplation of healing, with thoughts that promote healing, words that show belief in healing, attitudes that indicate you believe in the healing power of God.

Make a habit of assuring yourself of His healing presence and power by acknowledging it in specific words, by knowing moment by moment: *My healing is at hand. Thank You, Father.*

10

Refuse to entertain the slightest thoughts of lack of faith about yourself or another or the possibilities of healing. Refuse to give attention to discordant experiences or negative suggestions, knowing, instead, that healing is at hand. Accept it with praise and thanksgiving.

One person facing a life-threatening disease said that she found herself suddenly surrounded by those who believed that healing was at hand. Throughout the process of every form of treatment utilized—prayer, medication, biofeedback, laughter—the dominant thought was healing. Within a few months, diminution of the illness and a normal restoration of happy life activities were the result.

A young person who had been given a verdict of but a short while to live also found that healing was at hand. He was guided to seek another medical opinion. Later he wrote, "Many tests were administered and the results were negative, and reflected normal cellular structure. We were speechless! The physicians rationalized that there had been an error in the prior laboratory work procedure. We may never know what occurred technically. All the people and facilities were of the highest caliber." His healing was at hand.

Yet another correspondent shared, "A torn ligament in my knee brought about the discouraging feeling that it would never heal. Adding to this, I became ill with the flu. Desperately I turned to insisting, within myself, upon believing in the healing power of God at work in everything happening. It took wrestling with my thoughts, turning them toward faith again and again, affirming healing. Sometimes my efforts seemed mechanical; sometimes they seemed to contain merely a small growing conviction, but I kept on and on. Finally and suddenly, total wholeness came through! Thank God, healing was at hand!"

Your healing is at hand! Wherever you are, God is. Wherever you are, your healing is. God's love will never fail to enfold and protect you, lift and encourage you. God's love will never fail to show you the solutions to your problems, the answers to your dilemmas or confusions about life. Healing is everywhere and in everything! It fills the universe about you. It dwells in the kingdom of God within you. Wherever you sit or walk or work or live, your healing is.

You are a child of God, meant to express healing in every facet of your life and being. You are the offspring of Spirit, of wholeness and well-being, inheritor of the right to claim and accept any and every kind of healing needed. You were created with wholeness as an in-

12

nate reality of your identity. You have it within your soul and mind and body even when you seem to be unaware of it consciously. Yes, even in the midst of the challenging aspects of disease or disastrous happenings, healing is there. Your birthright of healing is adequate for every circumstance of life, for every demand. Healing is God-in-action in all creation, within you in this moment!

Let the word *healing* run as a golden thread extending to every distressing ache or pain of mind or body. Keep your inner eye upon this shining reality until everything within you vibrates to its silent presence within your heart. Charles Fillmore, co-founder of Unity, writes: "Health . . . is the normal condition of man, a condition true to the reality of his being. The first step in all spiritual healing is the using of faith, and the next step is to become open and receptive to the stream of healing life."

Use the faith you have at hand now, knowing that your healing is at hand. Practice repeating the words: *My healing is at hand! I accept it now with praise and thanksgiving. Thank You, Father.* Let the simple word *healing* dominate your daily thinking, and claim it as yours to have and to hold and express. Immerse yourself in thoughts of healing, and saturate your thinking with its meaning as given by the healer of every ill, Jesus Christ. Let it become more important to you than any negative aspect of any kind in yourself or another.

Healing is available to you, the Father's child, right now. Contemplate healing. Visualize healing. Work diligently with every manner and method of healing that encourages your conviction. Give praise and thanks that every healing you have ever desired is at hand! Be still and take time to listen within for directions as to the best way to accept your healing. Be obedient and follow the smallest light you glimpse. Follow the inner impulses that come to you, regardless of how inadequate they seem. Exercise momently your faith in the idea of healing and cultivate cooperation with God, the source of all wholeness and well-being.

Take time often to think about the words of Jesus of Nazareth, "If you have faith as a grain of mustard seed, you will say to this mountain, 'Move from here to there,' and it will move; and nothing will be impossible to you" (Mt. 17:20).

Remember, the mustard seed evolves, unfolds, to become a plant. This indicates that the faith seeming too small to be productive, too fragile and insignificant to bring about anything worthwhile, is the beginning of the wonderfully developed faculty through which the Father will work to bring about the wholeness you seek. Stay open and receptive to this idea and its possibilities, and, indeed, "nothing will be impossible" as His work of healing continues within you.

Hold close the wonders of wholeness and contemplation of healing until you see them dissolving every old habit of doubt and disbelief. The Lord of healing came, lived, and demonstrated healing of everything for your benefit, to assure you that nothing is impossible when you grasp the thought of healing and cradle it within your heart. No matter how much struggle it takes to return again and again to faith in healing, keep on returning. You may at times think, "I can't do it. There is no way. It will never come. It is no use." And yet, for every such negative protest, affirm again the positive conviction: *My healing is at hand!*

Pursue it until the light comes through and the inner peace is felt. Refuse to gauge your encouragement by any outer signs of progress or lack of it. Turn away from looking to see if the demonstration is happening as you think it should. Instead, focus totally upon healing, as you can best do so, until your interest is caught. Be held by a growing awareness of the omnipotent healing power of God in you and in all. Give thanks for the Christ way and truth and life of healing, for the gift of healing that rests within the deepest recesses of your soul, awaiting release and expression in your life.

To add to your reassurance and encouragement, use the meditation: *My healing is at hand. It is nearer than breathing, closer than hands and feet. It is all-present and ever available, abundant, and plentiful. It is here right now, wherever I am. It is mine without stint, mine without pleading or begging. It is mine to quietly accept, to bring me peace, assurance, and blessings beyond measure. Its source is God, my Father. That source never runs dry, never is lacking, never withholds, never denies. It is the same yesterday, today, tomorrow, and forever. It is within me every moment. I praise and give thanks for this reality.*

This meditation has helped me throughout the testing time of my own personal challenges. It has given me tracks to run upon when things have been difficult. It has given me the incentive to remember that healing is the will of God; healing is the desire of the Father for every child; healing will come through, even when it seems impossible to human reason.

It has lifted me over the hurdles and put my feet upon a rock of stronger belief and conviction in the unlimited presence and power of God. It has held me in the gentle softness of love when the human hurts grew painful. It has

16

healed emotions and body, as well as affairs of life. It has helped to heal those around me in need of ease and wholeness. It has charged and recharged my own growing faith and brought security within, again and again.

Your healing is at hand! Work with the idea of it as your very own. Know that it cannot be hindered, delayed, or taken from you by anyone or anything, at any time in your life. Healing is always there, where you are, and wherever you will ever be.

Healing is yours. Reach up now in your mind and heart to accept it and praise the giver of all wholeness and well-being—God, our Father, who loves you and cares for you, and will never fail you!

"If you have faith and never doubt, you will . . . say to this mountain, 'Be taken up and cast into the sea,' [and] it will be done. And whatever you ask in prayer, you will receive, if you have faith" (Mt. 21:21-22).

God Is Strengthening You Now

"Fear not, for I am with you, be not dismayed, for I am your God; I will strengthen you, I will help you."
—Is. 41:10

If you feel that you have reached the limit of your strength, take heart and know that this is the moment you are entering into an awareness of the greatest strength of all—the strength of God, the source of all the power there is. God is strengthening you now!

This source, ready to release its infinite and magnificent might, is available to you and to everyone seeking renewal of heart and soul, mind and body. This vitalizing energy is a power for good, and only good, for yourself and others—a constant and unfailing flow of silent inner renewal for every demand life makes upon you. It is born of love, love of the Father for His created, ever desiring to bring to all His offspring greater wholeness and well-being, peace and stability.

This strength will lift you over any challenge,

18

make a way for you through any negative appearances, and supply you with a continuing vitalizing force for the accomplishment of the longings of your heart. Knowing that it is God who girds you with strength, you will have the courage to say no to doubts and yes to faith. Knowing that God is strengthening you now, you will consistently deny limitation any place in your thinking, and you will respond wisely to challenges. You can move through tests of heartache or loss with faith in the ultimate outworking of good for all. You will have increasing might to believe in yourself as a child of God, and to decree and persist in knowing your eternal connection with the Father and His kingdom of good.

There is no negative appearance of any kind that can continue to stand before you when you know: *God is strengthening me now*. Every destructive thought, feeling, or emotion must give way when confronted by the declaration: *God is my strength. He is strengthening me now*. God is the power to lift, heal, bless, transform, and order everything aright. God is the power to work within you, and within everyone and everything surrounding you. No external condition of any kind is greater than the power of God's love, knowledge, or works of good!

You are given the promise, "They who wait

for the Lord shall renew their strength"
(Is. 40:31). Throw the entire weight of your responsibilities, anxieties, and burdens upon that supporting Presence and Power—God—your Father, whose might will handle all things easily and well.

When the negative aspects of a difficulty influence you to rebel, to say, "But I cannot face another struggle; I cannot cope with things anymore; I can't trust anyone again; I don't have the faith and strength to try; I don't even trust myself," this is the time you will find even greater capabilities within yourself than you have ever known as you hold fast to speaking the words: *Thine is the power, Father. Thank You for strengthening me now.*

A friend shared recently, "I found myself in the hospital for three weeks, during which time I underwent a serious operation. When I came home, family and friends came to see me with long faces. I knew what they were thinking. Three months later, I was back in the hospital for another operation. Again, family and friends came to see me with even longer faces. I knew they thought this was the end. Every time I tried to do something, my hands and body would shake. One afternoon a dear friend came to see me and brought a little booklet for me to read. When I opened it, I read the messages assuring me that God was my 'instant, constant, and abundant help.' This was the message of the *Daily Word*, and the first time I had ever seen it. That was twenty years ago, and I have never been without it. I have been in the best of health all of these many years!"

The power and strength and might of the Father are available and ready to work within your life. God is the only true Presence and Power. No matter what others may say, no matter what the human verdicts, prognoses, symptoms, or appearances, when you stand firm in your knowing that God is the source of your strength, He is strengthening you now, you will stand upon solid ground, with deeper levels of stability and faith than you thought you possessed.

This is what the loving Christ came to teach, to show you how to trust again, believe again, move forward again. He has given you His example of living a life which says that in the midst of all the worst that circumstances and humanity can present, you can come through with greater-than-ever power and strength.

With every word He has spoken, He points out for you the greater self that is yours, that lies within and is just beginning to surface in your prayers and seeking. He reminds you that this self lives within you, that this son of God

21

self, this offspring of the Most High you have inherited in spirit and truth is you.

His tenderness, understanding, and compassion want you to rest from your dependence upon human laboring and struggle, and to awaken to a new ease in handling everything in your life.

By Jesus' examples of prayer, and looking always to the Father as the source and worker of every good work, Jesus calls for you to exercise your growing faith, your seemingly inadequate spiritual understanding, and to let this develop day by day, by following the smallest glimmers of light. He knows the abilities and potentials that lie within you, and He calls for you to keep on, step by step, following in His footsteps. He is always here with you, ready to stretch forth His helping hand when you slip or fall and to encourage you to pray again, trust again.

With His reassurance, you will realize that you are not alone, and that you will have His support, assistance, and guidance all the way. He is your Elder Brother, who knows and loves you and believes in you as His younger growing-up partner in life. Putting your hand in His, you will find new abilities of mind, heart, and body, to be called forth and used.

In the light of this personal support, take

hold of your affirmations. Pray with new confidence. Bless your mind and body, heart and soul, with new appreciation. Look upon others with new trust and in new fellowship. Look at everything with new perception, knowing that everything happening now is working for you and developing the strengths of the Most High within you, readying you to express them for the highest and greatest good of yourself and others.

Jesus showed the greatest strengths anyone has ever known. He showed strength of character, of purpose, of motivation, and of caring. Strength of mind was His, as well as amazing strength of heart and soul and body. His spoken word reached beyond those physically and immediately present—through the miles and the years—to lift, help, and heal all who were ready to receive.

His strength of faith held secure in every test presented by the doubting multitude. His strength of love surmounted all the vengeful thoughts, words, and actions of the disbelieving. His strength of forgiveness and compassion have extended through the passage of time and will continue lifting, helping, healing, and blessing all humankind. Such manifest and visible strength, power, and might were born of the inner man, the true God self and nature, the Son

23

of God heritage and awareness that He proclaimed belong to all. This strength was perfected day by day, and night after night, as He grew "in wisdom and in stature," because of His total dedication to God.

You have within you at this moment an indestructible and eternal connection with total strength and power. You may call upon it in every need of life and find it abundantly providing for everything good and desirable. As you daily recognize and accept this inner connection, praising and giving thanks for your oneness with God, you grow in ability to express and show visibly His goodness, beauty, and healing power.

I know it is not always so easy to hold fast when things around you seem to be falling apart, yet that is the moment when you can be the most acutely aware of your oneness with the Father and His unending support, might, and delivering power. At one period in my life, when the challenges seemed far greater than I could handle, I turned to the tremendous reassurance of the words, "Thine is the kingdom and the power, and the glory, for ever" (Mt. 6:13 AV).

Then, again accepting that the Father was somehow strengthening me anew, I began to give up all questions, all resistance, all rebellion, placing them in His hands to handle, to transform, and to bless. I determined that all I would see was God, His power, life, wholeness, and well-being in all. I chose to respond only to love and peace. Looking across an expanse of water reflecting the blue of the sky and the grace of the seagulls sweeping overhead, tuning in to the quiet about me, I spoke the words again and again: *God is strengthening me now*, and gave thanks that, in Truth, God is the only power within me and within everything. I gave thanks that the Father was at work within everything happening, and that He is always the unlimited, unceasing strength of my mind, feelings, and body temple. In some way beyond my understanding, I knew that God's strength would always be there, not only for me but for all those I love and care about, and for anyone, anywhere, at any moment of need. The demands at that time were wonderfully met, and in the days ahead the Father did, indeed, "bear" and "carry" and "deliver."

This is what our Master has taught, and what I truly believe is intended to be accepted by everyone in every experience of life. It is not always simple to know and accept, but the greatest strengths sometimes come not only through, but because of, the greatest challenges, and out of apparent weaknesses new

25

strengths are born.

You have this power and might within you as the focal point of God's love and eternal provision. As His child, loved and cared for forever by His love, you will never be without the strengths you desire. He will ever be the strength of your heart, and He will daily, momently, strengthen you with strength in your soul.

Yes! God is strengthening you now!

His Touch Is Everywhere

"He touched her hand, and the fever left her, and she rose and served him." — Mt. 8:15

"Then he touched their eyes . . . . And their eyes were opened." — Mt. 9:29-30

There is no hurt within your mind or soul or body that the touch of the Master's love cannot heal. His touch is everywhere — within the deepest recesses of your heart, within the outermost reaches of any physical experience. Wherever or whatever the cause of your dismay, discouragement, or fear, it is never beyond the healing touch of Jesus the Christ. His touch is everywhere.

The most complex and difficult situation is within His grasp to solve, and the most trying circumstance is within His ability to clarify and set right. The One who came to show you the way to spiritual dominion, the truth of your oneness with the Father, and the life to be lived with authority over every negative opposition ever presented, is always with you. His touch is everywhere! It is timeless, unbound by space, unceasingly bringing comfort, light, and heal-

27

ing to all who will acknowledge and receive it.

Through the acceptance of that powerful healing touch, you can find your own wholeness and well-being, handle every situation wisely and well, be capable and confident, patient and forgiving. You can let go of burdensome feelings and past emotional trauma; you can be peaceful, glad, and free!

Know right now: *Through the healing touch of Jesus Christ, I am whole and well and strong. His healing touch is everywhere.* Build momently your growing awareness of what this touch means to you personally. Realize that it is not a faraway happening, occasionally coming and going within your life; rather, it is a consistent and unceasing healing presence, penetrating and moving throughout your entire life and being, and within everything that surrounds you. His healing touch is everywhere!

I have found, again and again, that by holding fast to this strong declaration compatible with my faith in the life and works of Jesus Christ a greater awareness of healing is built within, and greater strength, wholeness and ability manifest as needed and desired.

Charles Fillmore, co-founder of Unity, claims, "As day by day I repeat and courageously live affirmations of Truth, I come to know that I am opening a channel of intelligent communication with the silent forces at the depths of being; thoughts and words therefrom flow forth, and I realize an entirely new source of power developing within me."

Begin now to open that "channel of intelligent communication with the silent forces at the depths of being" by knowing: *The healing touch of Jesus Christ is everywhere.* Look to the One who not only spoke of healing, but lived it, proved it, and left us clear and simple ways to follow and gain our own healings, answers, and solutions. Thinking of His healing touch will give you strength, help, and motivation toward healing and blessing that will lift you above the habitual acceptance of limitations you have thought were your natural heritage. His touch will show you your true inheritance as a child of God. He will show you the most powerful way to live, and the most loving, wise, and joyful way to express daily.

I understand how it feels when you are trying to have faith, when you are tested and feel so devoid of help, and when your heart calls out, "Where are You, God? Where is my answer, my resource and strength?" It is humanly normal to feel this way in times of stress and aloneness, and yet, the greatest experience of lifting up, of renewal of faith, will find its way to you, into your being and life, as you remember the touch of Jesus Christ is at hand.

Through the healing touch of the Master Healer, you can do what you need to do with new confidence and success. Turning your thoughts to His healing touch, your prayers will be more effective and productive of good. Placing your attention upon His presence, His touch, you will speak with greater calm and assurance and be a far better channel for help and blessings for those you love.

As you consider the many ways in which healing came about for those who sought His touch, you see it was without confinement or limit of any kind. In some instances it was through the spoken word only. In other instances it became manifest through simple obedience to His guidance. Again, it was visible through stepping into a pool, or through application of moistened clay upon the eyes. In the latter instance, this was the same clay that others had stood and run upon, scuffed with their toes, let run through their fingers. And you know, therefore, that it was His touch—His conscious oneness with the Father—that brought about the miracles of sight, hearing, speaking, and total physical wholeness. You see that His touch revealed that there is inherent wholeness and healing power existing within everything in the universe.

30

A friend seeking healing of a bodily ailment was told that surgery was the answer. Not yet inwardly satisfied, this young man thought more deeply about the healing touch of the loving Christ; he remained open and willing to follow the guidance as it was presented. He was led, unexpectedly, to a nutritionist and herbal specialist. With this assistance and beholding the healing touch everywhere, he accepted prayerfully this way of help and the doctor's approval. Within two months the severe pains subsided. Physical examination was again called for as a continuing healing guide, and the reports were "All is clear. No need for surgery."

His healing touch is everywhere! Through knowing this, you will begin to feel it within your thoughts, your emotions, and the cells, nerves, functions, and activities of your body temple. You will go anywhere, through any challenge, any experience, with the greater calm and inner assurance that His touch is there, that it is everywhere. You will begin to relax, to open up to the understanding that all you are doing is added, guided, and empowered with new measures of faith because His touch is at hand, helping and healing!

His touch is, indeed, everywhere! It is always strong and effective, powerful and productive.

31

There is nothing too difficult for His touch to set right, to order anew. His touch is extended to you and to everyone you love, in compassion and understanding, and it is a touch that comforts you constantly. His gentle presence, His powerful touch, is love that lifts and blesses you always, and it is available and at hand now.

You are not shirking your own responsibility to learn and unfold your spiritual capacities in this manner of prayer. Rather, you are rightly joining forces with the One who knows the way you can go to attain greater awareness of your closeness to the Father. His touch is everywhere. With this decree you unite your growing spiritual perception with His superb awareness of Father and Son, and the healing power wanting to be released in the mind, heart, body and life of everyone!

The healing touch of Jesus Christ is everywhere! This is not a mindless or magical incantation, but a wholesome and wise unifying of your trust with the fully developed trust of the Son of God. With this action you turn to His love and eternally offered help. You receive the touch of greatness of the kind of faith to which you aspire. You accept your own spiritual heritage in the knowledge that you are, indeed, joint heir with Him and with all He is.

You can feel this reassurance of His help and

support in a multitude of ways. His touch of love often comes at first as a whisper, as a sudden stillness within that brings release from all turbulence of thought and emotion.

A person I know has an amazing rapport with butterflies. Wherever she goes, they seem to find her and hover about, alighting upon her. Other people may be standing close by, yet the butterflies are drawn always to her. She has written lovely children's stories on the subject, studied and loved the butterflies' fragile beauty, and they respond to her, seek her out.

One morning in a high mountain area, a group of us stood looking in awe at the beauty of the scenery far below—not a sound of birds or wildlife disturbed the quiet. Yet, within a few moments, a lone butterfly fluttered swiftly to my friend's side, alighting peacefully upon her hand.

Just as gently and quietly, you can become aware of the ever-present, ever-constant healing touch of the Christ. Knowing: *The healing touch of Jesus Christ is with me always; it is upon me now; it is everywhere*, you will find, in some wonderful way, that where you are His presence is. In some manner, encouragement will come as you have needed it. Somehow the Father's love will be revealed, bringing the upliftment, light, and healing you seek.

Another friend, a gentle young man who loves animals and birds, was recently at work inspecting the building of a modern high rise. He was standing atop the rafters on the ninth floor of the structure. Out of the corner of his eye, he saw a beautiful white cockatoo perched at the edge of the flooring. As he continued about his work, he suddenly felt a light touch upon his shoulder. The cockatoo had been drawn to him without hesitation, and peacefully remained there even as the young man traveled on about his chores, finally going down the elevator shaft, into his car, and home!

In a similar and lovely way, the healing touch, the healing presence of the Christ, is always seeking you out, ready to gently touch your mind with His light, touch your heart with His peace, touch your body temple and your life with His healing power. Wherever you are, even at times seemingly isolated from persons or things familiar and dear, you will find His touch there. Whatever your physical environment, regardless of how strange or foreign it may seem to you, even there you will feel the Master's touch of reassurance. It may come in a very simple or unexpected way, yet it will come. You are never beyond His presence and care, His touch and strength. Wherever you are, His touch is.

The healing touch of the Father, at hand now through the teachings, works, and presence of Jesus of Nazareth, the manifest Son of God, is now upon you, calming every fear, releasing every tension, uplifting your faith, setting aright every function of your being and your life. Be still, and give thanks that His touch is everywhere, that it is now upon you, within you, around you.

"Whither shall I go from thy Spirit? Or whither shall I flee from thy presence? . . . If I take the wings of the morning and dwell in the uttermost parts of the sea, even there thy hand shall lead me, and thy right hand shall hold me" (Ps. 139: 7, 9-10).

Your Trust in God Is Justified

"Those who trust in the Lord are like Mount Zion, which cannot be moved, but abides for ever."—Ps. 125:1

"Thou dost keep him in perfect peace, whose mind is stayed on thee, because he trusts in thee. Trust in the Lord for ever, for the Lord God is an everlasting rock."—Is. 26:3-4

Do not be afraid to place all your trust in God. Trust about your dear ones, your work, your relationships, your guidance in decisions, your healings of mind, emotions, or body— your total life! Your trust in God is justified.

He who created the universe and all that lives therein, who brought forth the vastness and order of the planets that spin in space, who designed the beauty of the blossoms that push open their delicate petals in the frosty spring— the Maker of all heaven and earth is worthy of your faith, worthy of your absolute trust!

The Father of all, who has made you in His likeness and in His own image and who has fashioned your mind to think through, your soul to love through, your body to move and express through, is the Presence and the Power upon which you can rely, upon which you can throw every weight of doubt or fear, every burden of life and being. Not only is He the originator of all creation, but God is ever the sustainer and upholder of all He has envisioned and brought forth.

Trusting in God in every detail of your life and affairs brings His love for you where He wants it to be—into the smallest routines of your days, into your office and home, into your labor and leisure, into every minute, hour, activity, and pursuit.

Trusting in God in every detail of your life brings His light and wisdom and healing where it belongs: under His loving guidance! And the more consistently you bring that presence consciously to mind, into your words and actions, being and living, the more powerfully He can benefit all the issues of your life!

Know, right now: *My trust in God is justified. Yes, Father, I am trusting.* As you take this step of firmly believing, you consciously permit strong development of the natural spiritual union of Father and child, Creator and created—God and you! By taking His presence regularly into your thoughts and letting Him move through you as the source of your life expression, every phase of worldly experience is charged with greater depth of meaning and blessing!

Not long ago, a friend needing financial help was assured on the telephone, "Your trust in God is justified. He will provide." This affirmative thought quickly provided her with a strong foundation of renewed trust in the presence of God, and she wrote, "My needs were immediately met. The very afternoon before my next morning's early departure, a gentleman appeared in the management office and immediately sublet my place for four months, with an option for five months. The interesting part of this is that he had approached the office a month ago but showed no interest in seeing an apartment."

Another friend, seeking support for increased faith when his faith was lagging, asked for a helping hand in prayer as he faced the challenge of the appearance of lung cancer. Prayers of several people close to him bolstered his conviction that his faith in the healing power of God was justified. He was encouraged to stand firm in this trust, knowing consistently, faithfully: *My trust in the healing power of God is justified*. A few months later, after another examination by the physician, he reported that the problem had resolved itself.

A young woman seeking to hold to the faith that it would be possible for her to bear a child in spite of several medical opinions to the contrary was reassured that with trust in God, *all* things are possible. She was urged to continue trusting. Within the year, a child was conceived and is now happy, smiling evidence of the all-present, all-fulfilling love of God.

Yes, *your trust in God is always justified in every way.* You can trust God to add increased health to your body temple, wisdom to your growing knowledge, and understanding of yourself and life itself—above and beyond that which you gain through normal channels of gradual personal growing and experience.

Jesus Christ is the supreme example of what trust in God—absolute faith in God—can do. He trusted God for every solution to every challenge in His life. He trusted His relationship with God to reveal all He needed to know and do in response to every demand of life or human need. He trusted the divinely planned kingdom within and the guidance of God, knowing that He had been given the innate ability to be a channel and a co-worker with God for the marvelous expression and manifestation of the goodwill of God for Himself and all humankind. His trust was justified again and again and again in everything.

His pure and consistently strong trust in and love for the Father needed no muscular strength to break through any physical barriers or walls. His absolute trust provided the channel through which every needed kind of strength poured quietly and effortlessly. From within a moment-by-moment, practiced trust in God, from an inner-listening quietness and confidence, arose every mental, emotional, and physical power and ability.

He could say, "He who has seen me has seen the Father" (Jn. 14:9), because of His recognition of total trust in God and because of His own indwelling Sonship. The strength of God, the love of God, the peace of God so filled the mind and heart of the Man of Galilee that His followers beheld God living in humanity—God working, walking, talking, and loving, and caring through us. This was a miracle-working relationship in action that needed to be seen so that each listener and follower could be elevated to a true vision and perception of what we are, too. Hear again His declaration to all who will listen: "Believe me for the sake of the works . . . . I say to you, he who believes in me will also do the works that I do; and greater works than these will he do" (Jn. 14:11-12).

You can trust this reality within yourself today. You can trust your own spiritual heritage, the Father working through you. Whenever you begin to feel unsure of the future, unable to face or meet the demands of the present, unhappy about yourself or the circumstances of life, know that this is the time for further development of your innate trust in God. Know that there are steps you can take humanly and consciously in union with the Presence and Power.

There are ways you can begin to cooperate with God's desire for your wholeness and well-being, strength and wisdom, peace and love and fulfillment. You can tell yourself, in fullness of trust: *Heaven and earth, all the powers of good that be now unite in healing me (or thee).*

Sometimes such a statement is needed to arouse the "adrenalin of spirit" to sweep away accumulated clouds of doubt and fear about yourself and your life. Years ago while attending a retreat at Unity Village, I heard a much-loved teacher give a series of lessons encouraging the use of the spoken word of affirmation along with physical exercise. His powerful voice and enthusiasm acted as a catalyst to arouse dormant faith and confidence and seemed actually to penetrate the very cells of the body as well as of the mind.

His message was a *summoned*, strong injec-

41

tion of the truth of being: It was needed to jolt the participants out of any passive mental attitudes they may have had. It was a reminder that there is something alive, real, and trustworthy about God and about our spiritual essence. It helped me, at that time, to realize that in spite of my human doubts and questionings, I could trust in God and trust His presence in me to express and live and move and act and be!

When you feel inadequate, unable to face life, remember that you can turn to the spirit of God within you and speak the words of faith needed to arouse any dormant ability. By speaking words aloud, and then becoming quiet and listening within, you will, in some way, be assured that the Father is responding to you, telling you, "Through my spirit in you, my beloved child, you can do whatever you need to do. You can be as strong as you need to be. You can be as unafraid as you desire to be. You can face every life experience in the knowledge that your trust is justified. I am here. I am with you always. I will never fail nor forsake you. Call and I will answer. Ask and I will give. I am your solid foundation to stand upon. Trust in me for every need in your life."

Even though you may not see how things can possibly work together for good, keep trusting

God. Trust the teachings of the Master of life, Jesus Christ. Trust His words, works, and His miracles. Trust His encouragement to you, telling you that you, too, are the "light of the world," the "salt of the earth." Trust that He knew what He was saying when He believed you could follow Him. Let your light shine.

By continuing to place your trust in God, your faith will wax strong, and your understanding of the power and effectiveness of God within you will support your efforts and fortify your awakening beliefs in yourself as a child of God. Yes, your trust in God is justified.

"Blessed be the Lord, my rock ... my stronghold and my deliverer, my shield and he in whom I take refuge" (Ps. 144:1-2).

You Deserve to Be Healed

"Fear not, little flock, for it is your Father's good pleasure to give you the kingdom."—Lk. 12:32

You, the Father's child, deserve to be healed, renewed, restored, revitalized, strengthened, peaceful, and whole. No matter how many contrary ideas may confront you, you deserve to be healed. As the offspring of the Father, as the recipient of His kingdom of goodness and all-sufficiency, you deserve to be happy and well and strong. You deserve to live and give and love, to receive and be blessed wherever you are, always.

At times human reasoning may try to convince you that you don't deserve God's help, that you have made too many mistakes, that God surely cannot care about you, that you are unworthy of His attention. Turn away from any such negative approach by reminding yourself that no matter what the circumstances, you are the Father's child. You deserve to be healed! As you remember this, you give the Father your full cooperation, saying "Yes" to His desire to help you, "Yes" to His longing to lift and renew you, "Yes" to His goodwill of healing! Accepting your indwelling worthiness as His beloved instantly erases any mistakes of the past, dissolves every feeling of inadequacy, and releases self-condemnation.

Jesus of Nazareth never would have been brought upon this planet to live the life He lived, to be the person He was, to heal as He did, to lift and supply and bless the multitude of so-called average humanity unless the Father had beheld the worth and value of everyone everywhere. The Master of life was aware of every need of those who sought His help, and His response indicated that individuals seeking improvement were deserving of it regardless of their backgrounds, imperfections of soul, or modes of living. He sat, ate, and communed with those scorned by their peers. He saw each person as a creation of value and encouraged all to seek the goodness of every facet of life because it was deserved.

Self-esteem was quickened and awakened within those who came before Him for help and healing. His presence brought about in them a new, strong feeling of worthiness, an awareness that it was right for them to be at peace and healed and blessed. He lifted their vision of themselves to a new dimension, to the recognition that wholeness was in order, that plenty was their heritage, that well-being was God's will.

This Man of Galilee told His followers, by word and by action, to claim the good that they deserved because they were the beloved of the Father. His kingdom was given to them. They deserved to be healed. They had a right to abundance, to all that was good, to the very best of life and living and being.

This bold attitude and acceptance of healing was based spiritually upon the reality of humanity's origin as the offspring of a living Creator, upon the inheritance of a spiritual kingdom standing behind every visible manifestation, upon the truth that spiritual law, God's law, forever substantiates and supports every good claim of His children.

No matter how long a person had believed in illness, in lack, in sorrow, or in unhappiness, the Master's message was always the same in essence: "You deserve the good you seek. God wants you to be whole." His followers were never told they were too old, too ill, too ignorant, too young, too human or too erring to receive the help they sought. Instead, they were encouraged to believe themselves worthy, urged to ask for fulfillment, even pushed and nudged to accept the healing of everything in their lives.

One of the most powerful, yet down-to-earth, parables the Way-Shower gave us, His listeners, was the story of the prodigal son, who had so lived his life that he seemed the epitome of unworthiness. He had so abused his inheritance, talents, and personal being that little hope existed for his rehabilitation. Yet, in this story, we are given absolute assurance of the magnitude of the Father's love and of our right to claim that which is always ours as children of God and heirs of the kingdom.

Another strong and clear message is found in John 20:24-30, which relates the unforgettable encounter of the disciple Thomas, known and remembered for his doubt about the reality of the Resurrection, with the resurrected Lord. Thomas is urged by Jesus—in a most dramatic way—to accept that reality. If ever anyone appeared undeserving of this opportunity and blessing, it would have been Thomas, the example of human stubbornness, disbelief, and doubt. Yet, Thomas is the one to whom Jesus chose to prove the miracle of the Resurrection.

He wanted all people to grasp the truth of the power of God inherent in them. He wants you, today, to accept your spiritual potential and value, to sense your capacity to be an active child of God, to experience the healing presence and power of the Father within your mind and body temple. He considers no one undeserving of the very best He has to offer.

He is saying, again, in effect, "You, as the Father's child, deserve everything good you desire: health, peace, love, joy, supply, all. What I have, you have. What I am, you are. The way I live and work and have my being, you may live and work and have your being. So, follow me. You deserve everything good."

Oh, yes, I know that when you are facing a challenge, it is not easy to remember that you deserve the relief and help and healing you desire. Your self-worth is, at times, deflated. Your value appears diminished. At times you feel you are sinking into a quicksand of self-pity and hopelessness. Yet it is vital, then more than ever, to remember that your spiritual worth is never changed, your value as a child of God is ever secure, and the kingdom of God within you is just as available and all-providing now as it ever, eternally, will be! God wants you to be whole. God wants you to accept the truth that you deserve to be healed!

The Father wants you to recognize and to accept your wholeness now. He wants you to behold the reality of His nature within you, to know firsthand the healing presence and power that lives within you. The life of Jesus Christ shows you that you are teachable and worthy.

At one time in my life when human losses seemed overwhelming, one thought sustained me: No matter what the happenings or the nature of the trial, and no matter what is required of me, God wants me to know peace, order, and total well-being within the experience. In the face of any feeling of aloneness, I deserve to know security. In the face of any appearance of discouragement, I deserve to know upliftment and reassurance. In the midst of any challenging emotion, I deserve to know peace and strength. God wants me to feel wholeness all the way through the experience.

These thoughts motivated me to accept more fully my spiritual birthright of serenity, faith, love, strength, wisdom, and even joy. It was a powerful realization to remember again and again: I deserve to feel the wholeness and healing of God. This remembrance strengthened me day by day, feeding and nourishing my thoughts, emotions, and body temple. It brought every detail, every action, every result under the abiding Presence. Unexpected and wonderful blessings and healings followed.

No matter how often you may get "off the track" of wholeness, God will lead you back. As you listen quietly, follow as well as you can. God will find a way to reach the most stubborn and rebellious areas of your mind, the most doubting and resistant places of your soul. Wherever you are, God is. Wherever you go, God will be.

Recently a friend shared that such thoughts had helped him through a period when he was undergoing some medical tests. He commented, "All the time I was going to the clinics and hospital to have these tests run, I absolutely hung on to the idea that through Christ, there is always healing mastery. I know now that this is true, for my checkups have proved it and all is well." Through these words, my friend touched and beheld, within his heart, the reality of the Christ life and wholeness in himself.

In any challenge in which you do not appear to have the answers you seek, remember that you, too, deserve to experience wholeness. You, too, can step beyond every personal doubt, boldly knowing that you have a right to healing, that you deserve healing, that you are worthy of healing. You, too, are to behold and say, with Thomas, "My Lord and my God."

Reach within yourself now to touch and feel and know that God's presence and healing power are here, where you are, and that you are worthy of accepting it in the way that is right and good for you. As you continue to give thanks for your heritage, the ways and means for your healing will open before you.

Hold to the thought: *I am deserving of everything good. As the Father's child, I deserve to be healed.* Put aside every doubt or fear. Step forward with new boldness and insist on your right to claim and experience the good you seek. This is your birthright. This is your heritage. This is the purpose for which you have come into this life experience. This is the time for you to touch God within yourself. This is the will of good for you.

Jesus came that you might have life more abundantly, that you might find wholeness of being, richness of life, and innate worth as a child of God. All His teachings point to your worthiness of well-being. He urges you to claim, accept, and give thanks for that heritage and for the wholeness that is yours. He is assuring you through every parable, through every example, that wholeness is the desire of the Father for everyone.

"Then he said to Thomas, 'Put your finger here, and see my hands; and put out your hand, and place it in my side; do not be faithless, but believing.' Thomas answered him, 'My Lord and my God!' " (Jn. 20:27-28)

Rise Up in Majesty

"Gird up your loins like a man; I will question you, and you declare to me. . . . Deck yourself with majesty and dignity; clothe yourself with glory and splendor." — Job 40:7, 10

There is a glorious and majestic presence within you. You have the qualities of greatness and honor, of fineness and nobility ready to unfold. There is a holy and wonderful Self contained within your soul, wanting to express. This Self is your child-of-God identity, the true and natural and normal child of God you were created to be. Rise in the majesty of your divinity now.

Nothing can destroy this reality. There is no circumstance or condition or personality or happening that can dim the brightness of your true Self. No matter how difficult your life appears, no matter how many setbacks occur, no matter how often you feel discouraged or unhappy or "put down" by anyone or anything, the majesty of your spirituality will rise above it all with overcoming power as you quietly decree: *I rise up in the majesty of my divinity now.*

52

As a child of God, you are stronger than any human weakness, more loving than any hurt feelings, greater than any fear, wiser than any dilemma, and completely peaceful in the midst of every confusion. You have within you an indestructible Self, a buoyant and resilient nature, an eternally forward-moving soul geared to surmount any challenge life may ever present.

There are within you resources of intelligence, vitality and energy, knowledge and wisdom, and life and healing that you have not begun to discover and tap. These resources, named the kingdom of God within you, await your recognition, acceptance, and use.

This is what Jesus Christ came to tell you and show you is your heritage. All that He expressed and proved through the daily working of miracles among the multitudes presents a clear picture of the true nature of humanity. His strength and love, His compassion and faith, His command and power, His gentleness and understanding give evidence of what God-in-us is like.

His answer to the Pharisee's question regarding His identity, "If you had known me, you would have known my Father also" (Jn. 14:7), was a forthright and bold declaration, reminding every listener that the Father lived and

53

moved within Him. Though Jesus no doubt knew that their disbelief would cloud their hearing and seeing of the truth about who and what He was, He rose in majesty and did not hesitate to declare it.

He reminded those who would and could hear what He was saying that the delight of the Father is to express Himself, to walk and talk and live and move, in His own created image and likeness—His offspring. Jesus of Nazareth was the powerful channel through which the Father could perform the works of His will of wholeness and renewal, provision and rich supply, love and wisdom and peace. This was His beloved Son who proved clearly the will of the Father for all.

Jesus Christ not only showed powerfully the image and likeness of the Father to all who chose to behold it, He also brought the directions and gave the rules for attainment of expressing Sonship, for rising in majesty and honor as the heir to the kingdom of God.

Through His knowledge and personal daily application of these rules, He produced results that no one before Him had been able to do fully. His dedication was complete. His obedience was absolute. His trust in God was implicit and unshakable. No matter how many refused to accept His ways, or condemned them, He stood firm. Regardless of every opposition, He persisted in awareness of His identity. In spite of every human activity or power used against Him, He kept rising in majesty.

The struggles of Jesus of Nazareth are described vividly, whether in the wilderness of temptation, facing crowds of disbelievers, the grief of losing someone He loved, or the darkness and solitude of Gethsemane. In each instance of trial and testing and temptation, His attitude, His direction, is evident: Always, He turned to God and followed God's guidance.

No matter what the situation called for—courage, faith, healing, poise, confidence, or inner peace—He counted on God to provide it without fail. Jesus knew that there was nowhere else He needed to turn, no person to whom He needed to look, no other source to draw upon for that which He desired. He plainly acknowledged the one true Source—the Father abiding within.

In majestic Sonship, He would declare, "I and the Father are one" (Jn. 10:30). To the Pharisees, He could say, "I have power to lay it [my life] down, and I have power to take it again . . . . Even though you do not believe me, believe the works, that you may know and understand that the Father is in me and I am in the Father" (Jn. 10:18, 38). He further declared, "All that the Father has is mine" (Jn. 16:15). This amazing strength of conviction and authority came from an awareness that the source of everything He would ever need came from one only, the Father of all—indeed, our Father.

Jesus relied completely and always upon God to show Him what to do: how to handle the "impossible" situations, cure the "incurable," and provide for every fulfillment of life. Whether for Himself and His own needs or for His followers and their needs, the source was always the same—His explanation was always the same: "I do nothing on my own authority" (Jn. 8:28), or "The Father who dwells in me does his works" (Jn. 14:10).

He rose in the majesty of His divine Sonship by allowing the Father to take over in every detail, and He always gave the glory of that rising to God. The credit and honor were given to God working within.

Again and again, the directions and the rules for His attainment were simple. He talked with God, aloud at times. He continually listened within for answers. He prayed and then followed obediently and thankfully the guidance given Him.

There was nothing shadowy, hidden, hesitant, or unsure about His manner of cooperation with God. He spelled out everything by word and action. He said, in effect, "This is the way the miracles happen. Do as I do, and the results will come." He consistently and continually rose to acknowledge the majesty of His identity and urged everyone to do the same.

When negative influences appeared from within or without, as they did, He again recognized His heritage and rose in mind and heart to the presence and power of God with and within Him. When He was faced with anger, sorrow, or disappointment, as He was, He again rose up above human dismay, recognized His reality, and moved ahead in the faith that the greatness of God within Him was more than equal to the demand.

Coming through human birth into the world of experience, you are given opportunity upon opportunity to learn and grow and understand the laws of Spirit and the majesty of your own being as the Father's child. Your human life is a vehicle through which the lessons are presented and through which your strengths are opened and more fully developed and manifested.

Whatever your challenge, by remembering your innate majesty you will move through every experience assured that the greatness of God within you will support you and provide totally and abundantly all that you need and desire.

As you decree: *I rise up in the majesty of my heritage*, you will find yourself aware of new dimensions of peace, strength, poise, power, and love. You will grow in your acquaintance with the Father abiding within, with His presence and power doing the good works through you that are to be done.

There is no need for you to cower or cringe in fearfulness or timidity before any situation in life. Rise up in the majesty of your divinity and give thanks that the Father abiding within you is giving you the wisdom to handle each detail wisely and well.

God Is Supporting
Your Every Effort

*"With men it is impossible, but not
with God; for all things are possible
with God."* — Mk. 10:27

When you feel alone in your search for
greater faith, to stand firm in facing a challenge, to keep on in courage, and believing in
healing of mind, emotion, body, or life situations, remember, God is supporting your every
effort.

Every prayer you pray, no matter how inef-
fective you feel it may be, is supported strongly
by God. Every decree you persist in making, every affirmation you speak in trying to hold to
faith in yourself or another is supported by
God.

The one Presence and Power is with you every moment, aware of your needs and desiring
to fulfill them. The healing Presence desires to
make known to you God's total and complete
approval of every move you make to help yourself. God is supporting you all the way.

When you think that you are at a stalemate,

59

that your struggles bring no desirable results, become quiet for a while and center your attention on the thought: *There is only one Presence and Power at work in my life: God, the good omnipotent. This Presence and Power is supporting me now. Thank You, God.*

You are not expected to solve any challenge by yourself. You are not created to live this life alone. There is an accompanying Presence and Power that is ever at hand to help you, to uphold you, to walk and work with you through every experience you face.

As you acknowledge this, your prayers and affirmations, your words and actions will take on a new expectancy and effectiveness, and any tensions or anxieties about the results will be released. You will become more and more aware that you have a partnership that, though invisible to human sight, is more tangible and real, present and powerful, than any outer help in all the world. You will feel the Presence and Power within your heart. You will know this Power is guiding you, is with you always, to do what you cannot and need not any longer try so hard to do yourself. Let go and let the supporting love and might and peace of God work in and through you.

When you are immersed in the negative aspects of a challenge, the process of "letting go and letting God" may take a while to develop and come to fruition. Jesus gives the parables of the ears of corn and the grain of mustard seed to remind you that there is an orderly process of fulfillment of healing of anything in your life, just as there is in the natural, visible world of growing plants.

This does not mean that the process of any healing takes three or six or twelve months to fulfill but that producing your good desires is based upon a law of step-by-step unfoldment. As in the instance of the miracles Jesus performed, results were often, in human time, instantaneous, and at other times not. Yet, in each instance the *process* was acknowledged and fulfilled.

The order of these steps always was followed clearly as by the Master. He turned from the problem to the Solver of everything. He kept His vision steady and gave thanks to the One doing the work. The words He spoke and the action He took varied from one circumstance and method to another, but the spiritual basis and principle did not. It was consistent, and the results were equally so!

There is only one Presence and Power in my life, my mind, my body: God, the good omnipotent. He is supporting me now. Thank You, God. Voice this idea to help you turn away from any

61

negative appearances. Repeat it to keep you steady in your faith. Give thanks to the One who is the only worker of any miracle. This is the orderly spiritual process that will bring the equally orderly unfoldment of good that is desired.

Regardless of the millions of varieties of plants that grow within the earth's appropriate soil, the process of growing is always the same, "first the blade, then the ear, then the full grain in the ear" (Mk. 4:28). And no matter what problem you may ever face, the process of solving, healing, supplying anything is always the same. The words of your prayers may change and your outer steps and actions may differ, but the spiritual basis does not change.

If you seek healing, know: *There is only one Presence and Power in my body temple: God, the good omnipotent. He is supporting me now. Thank You, God.* These words always help you turn away from the limited appearance and will keep you centered in faith in the presence and power of healing at work within you. Thankfulness for this truth completes the cooperative process between you and God.

As you use this idea to establish and re-establish yourself in faith, the awareness you desire begins to unfold, the inner "growing" understanding begins to take place, and the transformation of the mind emerges in order. Throughout the activity of prayer, of daily keeping your thoughts turned to God instead of to the problem, of giving thanks even when you do not yet see even the first "blade" appearing, be assured that God is supporting your effort in every detail. He is with you in every positive thought you think, every constructive move you make. He is supporting your every good effort and desire! God, the good omnipotent, the greatest and only true power in all the universe, is backing you, upholding you, supporting you in every moment of time and learning and growing.

Recently I was reminded of this wonderful activity as I admired the beautiful staghorn fern growing around the trunk of a palm tree in the backyard of our home. Years ago this plant was given up by several nurseries, considered worthy of nothing more than tossing out, since there was no evidence of a root system to support its life and growth.

To this day, no one can explain how the roots finally appeared, how the plant not only survived but grew into a magnificent example of beauty and strength! Each time I see it, it seems to say to me, "Where there seem to be no 'roots,' God will provide." God is the support system for everything, always! He will do what you cannot. He will provide what you are unable to provide. He will "grow" the faith, the vision, the substance, the "blades" of understanding, the strength, the abilities you desire. Even when nothing appears to be there, God is there. You do not have to know how or when it will come. Just trust and lean upon God's supporting presence and power.

Just as this amazing plant has given me a reminder, time and again, when I have needed it, the Father will provide you by word or example, or by just a quiet revelation within your mind and heart, that which will help and support your tender shoots of growing faith. The universe is filled to overflowing with "help at hand," with strong and steady support for any lagging belief in yourself or your ability to surmount the challenges of life.

A tremendous backup system above and beyond the beautiful and orderly support system of this limitless universe is ever present. It upholds you when you cannot uphold yourself, providing all that is needed when you can no longer do anything on your own. The loving Father back of all creation stands by His entire creation unfailingly and forever.

Relax and rest in God. Trust anew His tender care and unfolding process for your good. Know again and again that there is only one

Presence and Power in your mind, body, and life: God, the good omnipotent. This Presence is supporting you now in every endeavor. Thank God that this is so.

The support you need right now will come quickly. It may come quietly as a small thought. It may come through a person or a word encouraging you to keep believing and trusting. It may come silently as the dawn, as a new light breaking through your listening and receptive heart.

Your support is assured with every prayer of faith you pray, with every step of courage you take, with every move forward you take toward the desire of your heart. There is no limit to the Father's support of His beloved. He is supporting you now. He will be with you always!

You are not alone. You are not doing the work by yourself. You are supported in everything good by the Father abiding within you.

The Battle Is Not Yours

"Fear not, stand firm, and see the salvation of the Lord . . . . The Lord will fight for you, and you have only to be still." — Ex. 14:13-14

"O our God . . . our eyes are upon thee. . . . Thus says the Lord to you, 'Fear not, and be not dismayed at this great multitude; for the battle is not yours but God's.' " — 2 Chron. 20:12, 15

Regardless of any multitude of challenges facing you, remind yourself: *The battle is not mine; it is God's.* Then let go and let God do all that needs to be done, within you as well as around you. His light will go before you to make clear your way. His power will move through you to give you courage and strength. His love will abide within you to give you peace and calm.

Wherever you go today, wherever you are — in the midst of any commotion or desolation, crowded by others or alone — be not afraid or dismayed. There is a Presence and a Power at work within your mind, heart, and body. There—in love and power, in peace and strength, with you and within every atom of your being—it is already in action, bringing about the best result for healing and supply for you and for all whom you love and hold dear!

Again and again this day, "hold your peace," then let go and let God, remembering: *The battle is not mine; it is God's.* Deliberately turn away from pursuing any limited thought or feeling, and speak the words quietly to yourself again: *The battle is not mine; it is God's.* Relax your anxieties; let them drop away. Let go all tension. Give everything into the Father's keeping, into His care and His love.

One of the most remarkable things about the Man of Galilee was the power He wielded over everything without lifting a hand or fist toward physical battle. Every opposition within and without totally was vanquished by an invisible might that moved silently to overcome the greatest enemies of the well-being of humanity. Whether the threat was to another, to Himself, or to the purposes, dreams and goals of His heart, He turned from resistance to rely upon the Father. He knew the battle was not His, but God's.

Because of His constant nonresistant attitude toward any negative appearance and His unvarying attention to the Father, all the evidence of built-up might of sword or missile, all the show of human force and domination was no match for the Son of God. No material armament could penetrate the security and safety of His life. All authority was given unto this One who knew the miracle-working power of nonresistance.

In urging His followers not to resist evil, He did not imply joining forces with the disastrous challenges presented. Rather, He encouraged them to turn all their energies of mind and heart to awareness of the reality of the presence and power of the Father. He wants you, too, to sense that presence, to behold that power, as He did, to keep turning to God only. He urges you to remember that the battle is not yours, but God's.

Ah, yes, skirmishes with life's facts are not easy to avoid when someone you love is enduring a difficult physical or emotional challenge. You naturally want to fight the battle with or for that person. You feel you must stand and defend and protect those you care about. You are ready to "do battle" with anyone or anything that threatens another or yourself. Your energy is geared toward action that supports what is right and healing and helpful and good for all.

Yet, the Master of all overcoming, through His words "Do not resist" (Mt. 5:38) and "Make friends quickly with your accuser" (Mt. 5:25) gives you a way to follow that is more powerful than any before known: nonresistance. This way seems, at first, to permit all that is "evil" and to annihilate everything that is good and worthwhile. Yet, this way allowed the One who followed it to perform unlimited miracles. Nonresistance to blindness brought sight to eyes that had not seen. Nonresistance to deafness brought hearing to ears that had not heard. Nonresistance to poverty and lack brought abundant supply to the multitudes. Nonresistance to incurable diseases brought wholeness and well-being to minds and bodies. Nonresistance to crucifixion and death brought resurrection and life.

As taught and practiced by this Healer, this attitude was not one of meek subservience to any negative circumstance, situation, or person. It was, instead, an all-powerful recognition that the battle, the overcoming, belonged always to God. This perception did not ignore the needs of the minds and bodies and lives and affairs of His followers. He beheld and knew — and was touched by — the afflictions of those who came to Him. But His eyes were predominantly upon the ever-providing, ever-loving,

69

and powerful presence of the Father. This was the dominant thrust of His attention.

This consistent and constant turn of His thoughts and feelings was practiced. It was a day-by-day, night-by-night, moment-by-moment discipline. It was a trained, quick turning of attention from a natural human rising in anger over injustices to a calm awareness that God would bring goodness and healing into the very spot where injustice existed. Regardless of the nature of the difficulty, who had caused it, why it had occurred, and how impossible the solution appeared, He responded not with rebellion, argument, fighting, or resistance, but with a strong focus of attention upon the knowledge that the work was the Father's, not His.

He knew that this practice and discipline would not come easily to His disciples, so He gave them, through His teachings, practical examples of how to agree with the adversary quickly. He said specifically and clearly, "Don't fight, don't argue, don't rebel, don't resist. Just keep trusting the Father. Put all your attention upon His presence and power, as much as you can, as often as you can, in every way that you can."

He is telling you, today, not to divide your seeing and hearing between what is happening and the presence of God. Instead, practice and train and discipline your thoughts and feelings, words and actions, until they habitually turn quickly and consistently to the one Presence and Power—God abiding within. He is saying, "Remember, the battle is not yours; it is God's."

Not long ago, a friend found himself in the grips of fear and panic, struggling to find an answer to a tragic challenge facing family members dear to him. For weeks he seemed unable to pray, caught in a web of rebellion against the circumstances. Later, he commented, "I could find no relief for myself mentally or emotionally until I came across the words in a Unity booklet, 'Stop struggling. Of yourself you can do nothing. Let go, and let God do the transforming within you. Let Him mold your consciousness anew.' In that moment I realized I needed to, and could, release and let go to God all the adversaries of thought and feeling. I was at peace, and that peace has sustained me throughout and brought me the understanding I needed and the answers that followed." The battle is not yours, but God's.

Another friend shared, "In a recent challenge in the life of a person very dear to me, my emotions of concern and anxiety became involved deeply. In an hour of desperately seeking for guidance to know what I could do to help the situation, the words 'Let my children go' came to me softly but distinctly, as though spoken aloud.

"I sat back, almost with shock, at the implication and realized in that moment that my rebellion and anxiety had been overshadowing my ability to release and trust. I had begun to take upon myself burdens of responsibility that I could never solve or heal, that were, in fact, God's to handle. I knew then that my angry resistance would never win the battle. It would be the Father abiding within each dear one who would do the work and bring the light needed."

Within a few days, this person learned that the answers were already on the way for those she loved and that the healing already had begun. God was already there, in control, at work.

There is no dimension of fear, trauma, emotional confusion, or mental anxiety that can obscure the presence and power of God when you persist in turning to face it with trust and with willingness to let all else fall away. God's help is always at hand. God's reassurance and power and action are always in motion. No matter how many "demons" of panic seem to want to frighten you or how many "ghosts" of disbelief appear, remember, the battle is not yours, but God's.

You are not without a choice as to where to

place your attention at any moment or in any experience. As you turn again and again, as often as you need to do so, to the presence and power of your Father, you will feel calm, courageous, strong, and convinced that everything is already working toward healing, that God is already "fighting the battle" for you, and that His overcoming is assured.

You are a co-worker with God. There are always steps to take, moves to make, prayers to pray, and affirmations of healing and faith to be proclaimed. Yet, remember that your endeavors are not the working agent for solution; they are merely the door opening to your mind and heart so that God can freely flow through you to bring about the good you seek.

God knows how to do whatever needs to be done, so release and trust. God is ready to act for you as you let go. Begin now the harmonizing, cooperative process, for anything in your life needing healing, knowing: *The battle is not mine; it is God's.* Praise and give thanks to the Father for the healings that are already on the way.

Turn Everything to Praise

"It is good to give thanks to the Lord."

—Ps. 92:1

"Rejoice in the Lord . . . and give thanks." —Ps. 97:12

"Enter his gates with thanksgiving."

—Ps. 100:4

When you have reached any point in your life that seems insurmountable, turn to the greatest key given by every worker of miracles known: thankfulness and praise to God. No matter how solid or unyielding the wall of difficulty before you, praise will bring brightness, light, and understanding. No depth of despair or lack, no other "creature" of thought or threat of destruction can stand against the mind and heart that has set itself to sing praises to God consistently, giving thanks and all glory to Him.

Praising the Father wholeheartedly lifts the soul to a new concept of the presence of God at work. Praising the presence of God everywhere and in everything causes all circumstances and things to respond with miracle-working cooperation and harmony.

Instead of waiting to give thanks until the fulfillment you seek becomes present and visible, begin now to praise God. Build the habit of saying, "Thank You, God!" morning, noon, and night in every instance where remembrance of His presence is needed. When your prayers seem effective, and when they do not, voice the affirmation: *Thank You, God*. Whether you feel "up" or "down," encouraged or dismayed, again decree: *Thank You, God*. Whatever your mood or challenge, turn it all—every emotion, every thought, every word, every action—to praise, praising God in everything. Begin now to turn everything to praise.

During a time when I felt challenged by a series of negative events, I attended a concert by an entertainer well-known for his unique piano arrangements of the composer Gershwin. His artistry was enhanced by the accompaniment of a band of young student musicians and faculty members. For two hours the lively, powerful, and joyous strains of beautiful music filled the air, delighting several thousand listeners.

The vibrations of joy, love, life, and beauty were so overwhelming, so powerful, that time after time people stood in the aisles clapping and smiling in an outpouring of appreciation for the performance. A surge of energy not only permeated the atmosphere but also could be felt as a healing activity within the mind and body. It was a faithful accompaniment to the Psalmist's words, "Praise the Lord! Praise God in his sanctuary; praise him in his mighty firmament! ... Praise him with trumpet sound; praise him with lute and harp! Praise him with timbrel and dance; praise him with strings and pipe! Praise him with sounding cymbals; praise him with loud clashing cymbals! Let everything that breathes praise the Lord! Praise the Lord!" (Ps. 150)

For days after the concert, I could sense and enjoy the healing power of praise and joy that had emanated so naturally and freely from and through everyone joined in a spontaneous expression of thankfulness. The healing that I had sought and needed was experienced.

Little wonder that singers were appointed to go before the Israelite armies to strengthen their ability to protect their territory. No wonder psalmists met every challenge of life with song after song of praise to God, with thankfulness in spite of every difficulty, repeated and voiced unceasingly. Surely it was not strange that Jesus of Nazareth, the greatest of all miracle workers, standing as the example of the Son of God made visible, gave thanks even before the miracles of healing or provision were manifest.

Everything responds positively to prayer and praise! When "you are not conscious of having received anything from God, do not worry or cease from your thanksgiving. Do not go back of it again to the asking, but continue giving thanks that while you waited [in prayer] you did receive, and that what you received is now manifest; and believe me, you will soon rejoice and give thanks, not rigidly from a sense of duty, but because of the sure manifest fulfillment of your desire." (*Lessons in Truth* by H. Emilie Cady)

Sometimes praise flows easily, sometimes not, but persistence in thanksgiving is one of the most rewarding and powerful healing agents known. Turning everything to praise begins a lifting process of the mind. It regenerates the emotions and the cells of the body temple. Praise strengthens and energizes, empowers and invigorates all functions of your being. Turning everything to praise is a miracle-working process.

Some years ago when I was visiting with a dear one in an effort to help him through the loss of a beloved family member, I was aware of the heaviness, gloom and sorrow that filled the home. To the human heart, this was a natural state of feeling, but one not intended or in order to continue! Calling for guidance to know how best to bring a blessing to that household, I was moved to begin a silent activity of praise and thanksgiving within myself and within the room in which I was to sleep that night.

I softly but determinedly lifted my voice in praise and turned everything to thanksgiving. I praised and blessed the walls, the halls, the room, the furniture, the minds and hearts of everyone coming to mind, myself, my words, my faith. Although I knew I could not work a miracle, I believed that if I turned everything to praise, the Father would have His greatest opportunity to work His healings and blessings right there in the midst of the deepest sadness. By morning, at breakfast, the darkness that had been felt so heavily was gone. The atmosphere was one of peace and release. Praise somehow had opened the doors to healing and evaporated the shadows.

Don't be shy about giving praise and approval. Lavish your mind and body with praise. Pour "oils of joy and gladness" upon yourself from tip to toe. Pat your shoulders with loving kindness. Rub your toes with gentle encouragement. Massage your arms and legs with tender care, faith, and appreciation. In tones of quiet strength and upliftment, talk to the areas needing healing. Turn everything to praise.

Because of the body's involvement with the

limited ways of the world, you may at times barrage it with condemnation, for being too thin, too fat, too young, too old, too tall, too short. Added to this, you may indulge in critical self-analysis, "Why was I so thoughtless?" "Why did I say that?" "Why couldn't I have done better?" "Why can't I be more spiritual, more loving, more successful?" The heaviness of such thinking is like a blanket of disapproval thrown upon the mind and heart and body. It is enough to set the very cells into confusion and retreat.

Turn the tide. Turn everything to praise. Bless and bless and bless your body. It is God's holy temple. Tell it so. Bless it for being an obedient and willing vehicle created to serve you in this life experience. It deserves your daily positive thoughts and loving approval. It deserves to be praised, encouraged, nourished, and supported by your clearly directed love and wisdom.

Instead of focusing on imperfections of your mind or being, begin a flow of daily, regular messages of gratitude. Become a special friend to yourself. Befriend your mind with praise. Befriend your heart and your body temple in every step you take, in every move you make. Talk to yourself silently and aloud, giving thanks for every smallest ability to function, for every greatest desire to function better and better within this beautiful universe. Turn everything to praise and thanksgiving.

Use daily the following clear and specific prayerful exercise in praise as a basis to assist the healing process. Sit quietly and talk gently, but firmly and lovingly, to yourself: "Now hear this, (call yourself by name). You are the holy temple of the living God. Every cell, atom, muscle, nerve, every part of you from head to toe is a loving creation of the Father. You are, in God's sight, perfect, holy, harmonious. You are manifesting that real self now, in every function, action, and reaction.

"I praise and bless you and thank you for your faithful response to the spoken word of healing and strength, for your willingness to be a channel of God's will and works. I praise and give thanks that your source is God and that your resources of strength, recovery, stability, and well-being are infinite. You are under the constant guidance and direction of the Holy Spirit of love and wisdom, and you hasten joyfully to carry out every purpose and function obediently and well. I thank and praise and bless you. You are filled with the light, beauty, and glory of God, in whose image you are created. I now stand still in the midst of love and praise, beholding the presence of God within you."

Praise and give thanks and glory to God, the unfailing source of your life, peace, love, and wholeness. Turn everything to praise. Accept your inheritance of healing now.

"It is good to give thanks to the Lord . . . . For thou, O Lord, hast made me glad by thy work; at the works of thy hands I sing for joy" (Ps. 92:1, 4).

God Is Here Now

*"Behold, I am with you and will keep
you wherever you go . . . for I will not
leave you . . . . Jacob awoke from his
sleep and said, 'Surely the Lord is in
this place; and I did not know it.' "*
                                        —Gen. 28:15-16

God is here now. His presence as healing, peace, love, strength, and wisdom is not a figment of your imagination. God is real, present, available as the source of your being, as the inexhaustible fount of life and wholeness. His power upholds the earth in its orbit, performs the unfolding miracles of growth and fruition in all things and creatures, and enables you to think and to feel, to be and to experience positively every phase of life.

God is here now. More than you have yet conceived, God not only is your Creator, but also the sustainer of your identity as His child. God is all of this, and far beyond your highest contemplation. God is your all in all, now and forever. God is the source of supreme love, tenderest compassion, and untold beauty, joy, well-being, and inspiration, the wellspring of fulfillment for every good desire of your heart.

The One who knew the Creator intimately as "Our Father" brought the Father's reality into every simplest detail of living to show that God is not a God far from any of His children, but a presence and power "abiding within" them. He was saying to all that God is here now, in every way that you need Him to be in your life today and always.

God is ready to meet you where you are, in this moment, as the answer to any need for healing of body or soul or for guidance in either a small detail or a momentous decision. You are important to God because you are His image and likeness, created as God's channel of life expression. You are, indeed, the "light of the world."

The Master of being, Jesus Christ, gives not general but deliberately specific ways in which you may find a close relationship to God and complete oneness with the goodness of life. Jesus did not say that only some were to ask and seek and knock; He urged all, according to individual needs and desires. Anyone is worthy; anyone may ask and receive—anyone—in any stage of life and learning, regardless of race, personal background, age, social status, or education.

Regardless of your level of spiritual understanding, you have a right to know God, to communicate with God, to ask and receive, to accept every opportunity to experience your spiritual nature here and now. There is no reason, therefore, for feelings of loneliness or unworthiness. Understanding this draws you into the realization that you are always part of the goodness of God's world and its activity.

One of the most remarkable personal helps in healing came to me at a time when I needed to remember this truth. As I sat quietly in prayer, seeking guidance to help myself, to open my mind to a closer awareness of God, the thought came strongly and clearly: "Where pain, hurt, and fear appear, this is where God is to be made known to you. This is the very place to recognize, accept, and glorify God's presence within you, within this experience, within this challenge."

In that moment healings began, within and without, and continued for weeks in overflowing measure, reminding me again that God is here now.

One of the most powerful of all Old Testament stories substantiating the reality of God is found in the third chapter of Daniel. Shadrach, Meshach, and Abednego, three devoted followers of the one true God, refusing to bow in worship to King Nebuchadnezzar, were cast into the "burning fiery furnace" without hope of deliverance. In that moment, however, the story tells of the amazement of the angered king, who said, "I see four men loose, walking in the midst of the fire, and they are not hurt; and the appearance of the fourth is like a son of the gods" (Dan. 3:25). Then all "gathered together and saw that the fire had not had any power over the bodies of those men; the hair of their heads was not singed . . . no smell of fire had come upon them" (Dan. 3:27).

When your prayers and affirmations become the most powerful ideas in your mind, all that is to the contrary will give way, for then the Son of God is perceived, in control, and about the business of help, healing, and deliverance.

Jesus of Nazareth puts it very simply and plainly: "The eye is the lamp of the body. So, if your eye is sound, your whole body will be full of light" (Mt. 6:22). It also will be full of wholeness, peace, strength, protection, and deliverance from anything. Jesus knew this and proved it so that all could see the reality of the presence and power of God in all.

I once listened to some scientists explaining their search for information regarding the process of photosynthesis, the transforming of sunlight into life within green plants. The scientists demonstrated the steps of investigation—cut the plant leaves, chopped them into

85

small pieces and moved through the various stages of scientific experimentation until, finally, a small mound of plant leaves, placed in a container, produced a beautiful, soft-focused glow of light.

"You are the light of the world" (Mt. 5:14) is not merely a marvelous declaration of the greatness of spiritual potential within you. It is a scientific proclamation by One who knew the entire concept and reality of life. He led the way to all healing and unceasing life, knowing that the solid basis of all reality is God abiding within as the true light, substance, and life of everyone and everything.

This light cannot be hidden, destroyed or denied expression when acknowledgment of its presence is complete, when the eye of the mind and heart is single to its reality in any experience or happening. Every affirmative declaration, every prayer of praise and thankfulness toward this concept in some degree gives birth to the latent processes of activity always ready to reveal the light of the world in your life, in your circumstances, in your body.

Sometimes this realization is made known in an instant. At other times it seems to take more time, patience, and persistence than you feel you possess. Yet, with every effort you make, you grow in wisdom and stature, and more of the light begins to flow through you: I know such effort is not easy in the throes of fear, pain, panic, and despair. You long for relief to come quickly. I know that at times you want to get it all over with quickly. Yet, to gain at that time the concept that in the midst of the fiery furnace is the abiding presence of the Son of God, is to release all timing and results of manifestation of healing in favor of a miraculous experience in that moment where you are.

Perhaps Jesus would have preferred less than a long night of trauma in Gethsemane or less than three days in the tomb. Yet, in the midst of the dark hours of that lonely night and in the midst of the lonely days and nights in the tomb, life and light were active and miracles were happening. Devotion to the presence and power of God came—with practice—to Jesus, as it comes to you and me, through life's experiences and challenges.

It is in the midst of weakness that you are made strong. In fear-filled times you are given courage. In trauma you are brought into serenity. In discouragement you find faith.

God is here today, tonight, tomorrow, and forever. God is the light of your mind, body, and life, always.

Friends have shared with me that in the midst of challenges, they have seen the presence of the Son of God as strong and gentle and beautiful. Others have expressed that their healings came through in other ways—sometimes just as a strong and quiet thought, as a new idea received through reading a Unity message, through a loving and caring voice over the telephone, or through meditation with a friend or counselor. The spirit of God's love works in many ways to bring awareness and answers to prayer.

There is no need to struggle to achieve a particular way of deliverance, a certain manner or method of answer to your prayer. Rather, you can release the manifestation of the deliverance to the love and wisdom of God, and just know that God is here now. The ideas you need to help you behold God most clearly will be revealed. The way of seeing and hearing and touching God's presence and power will be brought into your mind and heart. Be still and know. Praise God's presence here with you and within you. Above and beyond anything you may experience, give thanks now that God's love and healing power are real.

Thank You, God, for Your Healing Light

*"And God said, 'Let there be light';
and there was light."* — Gen. 1:3

*"And without him was not anything
made that was made. In him was life,
and the life was the light of
men. . . . The true light that enlightens
every man was coming into the
world."* — Jn. 1:3-4, 9

If you are unable to find the right word to say
or the helpful action to take in seeking guidance and healing, begin to use the affirmative
prayer: *Thank You, God for Your healing light.*

Praise the Father repeatedly for His healing
light, and let it transform your thinking, calm
your emotions, direct your steps, and fill your
body temple with wholeness and well-being.

Thank You, God, for Your healing light. Let
this idea of healing light permeate your
thoughts, surround you with protection, and
guide your every step. Everywhere you go, everywhere you look, everywhere you are, give

thanks to God for His healing light.

No fear or distress can overpower this healing light. No darkness of mood or emotion can prevent its penetrating, healing presence. It can fill and bless every condition or situation, every emptiness or void. It can feed and nourish every hunger.

Begin to let God's healing light dominate your thinking and speaking and acting. Tell yourself that there is nothing but God's healing light. All that you know, see, feel, or experience is God's healing light.

Remember the words of Jesus of Nazareth, "You are the light of the world. A city set on a hill cannot be hid. Nor do men light a lamp and put it under a bushel, but on a stand, and it gives light to all in the house. Let your light so shine" (Mt. 5:14-16).

Now, boldly hold up your words of faith: *Thank You, God, for Your healing light.* Hold them high in your thinking. Lift up your voice clearly so that it is impossible for your declaration of healing to be missed within any area of your mind or body. Make your statements of trust in the healing light of God so obvious, so noticeable to yourself, so loud and clear that they will give new light to everything that lives within your house of thinking and feeling. Let them dominate, and help them to do so.

Yes, it takes exercise, knowing, believing, and devotion to build adequate faith when negative conditions of life challenge you. The master of light and life, Jesus Christ, knew this, and He did all that He asks you to do.

I once sat with a group of young, talented musicians after their concert performance for thousands of interested listeners. I was intrigued with the musicians' extreme devotion, with their total involvement with music. They lived and breathed and loved their chosen profession. They gave themselves to it completely. It dominated their every word and action. Amid the conversation that flowed about them, they seemed to hear only music. Nothing else spoke to them so loudly and clearly. They were centered joyfully and energetically in the dominant love of their lives.

A few days later a friend shared with me the following experience. A heavy trunk lid had been slammed down forcefully upon his hand, catching four of his fingers beneath it. Everyone around him had exclaimed in sympathetic pain and begun to rush about in panic. However, after the lid had been lifted, amazed onlookers saw only a flexible, perfect hand and undamaged fingers. My friend smiled as he related the incident, "There wasn't an instant when I was unaware of wholeness for my hand.

All I thought about, as a result of knowing this same truth many times before, was the constant presence of God's healing light. It dominated me completely in spite of all the commotion and confusion and negative responses around me." Like the musicians, my friend gave himself completely to what he loved, wholeness.

This is the reason for Jesus' parables of the "strong man, fully armed," guarding his palace (Lk. 11:21), or the vulnerability of the empty house "swept and put in order" (Lk. 11:25). You must be strong and diligent in keeping your thoughts full of the desired results. Dominance of healing ideas is an absolute necessity. This is what your affirmations can help you accomplish. This is why you declare: *Thank You, God, for Your healing light*, even when you do not know how it can happen and when all appearances may deny the possibility of healing.

You may need to repeat *"Thank You, God, for Your healing light"* many times during the day or night until you feel the stability of the idea. If you find yourself off the track, caught up in negative appearances, just turn back to the central idea you are wanting to experience and again affirm: *Thank You, God, for Your healing light.*

It makes no difference what challenges your

life presents to you. You can be assured that the light of God is great enough, powerful enough, to bring healing. His healing light is ready right now to gather you up into His love, to help you focus on the "true light that enlightens every man . . . coming into the world" (Jn. 1:9), to wipe away all disbeliefs, fears, and doubts, and to show you the wholeness already indwelling you.

As you relax now and accept God's healing light, everything in your life and being will respond to the gentle but powerful rays of God's love. Through God's love your own is amplified. Through God's power you gain awareness of your own authority. In the healing light of God, you can rest, trust, and find the healing you desire.

I understand that at times it seems you cannot see that light or feel it and that you wonder if the presence and power of God will ever become apparent through your struggles and efforts. Remember then that you are not walking your path alone. The love of God and of Christ is with you always. The light that showed so powerfully through Jesus Christ long ago is a light that found release through His life on earth so that it might be evident for all humanity forever.

Jesus' birth in Bethlehem was a point of such

clear release of light and healing that the heavens and the earth shone with a heavenly light that the shepherds could see. That healing light still fills this planet and surrounds you, where you are now, with peace and assurance as you become quiet and thankful and receptive.

The same transforming light the disciples saw on the Mount of Transfiguration is seeking to shine through you as you turn in prayer and let His healing light transform your fears to faith, your confusion to peace, your trembling to strength, and your every uncertainty to spiritual conviction.

The smallest flashes of insight you occasionally may feel within your mind or heart, the little awakenings of trust and faith you feel in prayer are the beginnings of revelation of the healing light. Praise and bless every smallest and most insignificant sign of any new understanding and clear vision. Give thanks to God again and again for His healing light at work.

It is God's desire that you see yourself as you are, whole and perfect as created by God. Cooperate now with this desire and decree again: *Thank You, God, for Your healing light in me.* Let this light be released through you in quietness and inner listening. Let it shine stronger and stronger within your smallest daily chores, and your greatest demands. Give thanks that it is being released even now, in this moment, as you speak the words softly: *"Thank You, God, for Your healing light in me."* Keep turning to that light. Keep letting it shine through. Every healing will follow!

"And as he was praying, the appearance of his countenance was altered, and his raiment became dazzling white. ... And when they wakened they saw his glory .... And a voice came out of the cloud, saying, 'This is my Son, my Chosen; listen to him!' " (Lk. 9:29, 32, 35)

You Can Understand

"Happy is the man who finds wisdom, and the man who gets understanding . . . . Long life is in her right hand; in her left hand are riches and honor. . . . All her paths are peace. She is a tree of life to those who lay hold of her; those who hold her fast are called happy."—Prov. 3:13, 16, 17-18

There is an understanding self within you that knows you are strong and powerful when everything human seems to say you are weak and inadequate. This understanding self in you sees you poised and confident when your every thought and emotion tends toward uncertainty and discouragement. This self in you understands that you are healthy and whole even when bodily aches and pains seem overwhelming.

The understanding self within you knows how to approach every challenge in wisdom and courage. This self within you always has been, is now, and always will be at one with God. This self supports you in your purposes in this life, viewing all situations from the standpoint of firm spiritual authority.

Your wise, understanding self knows all about negative confrontations and how to deal with them successfully and in peace. In every circumstance, this self is emerging into a greater degree of expression through you. It is your true, eternal reality, created and born of God.

Begin to acquaint yourself now with this self within you and be at peace. Be still and know that this self is awaiting your acceptance, ready to come into healing activity wherever and however needed. Give thanks for this self that is you, one with God, joint heir with Christ. This is your true, unfettered self.

Often take time away from outer demands and be quiet and alone, even if only for a few minutes. Talk to yourself by openly saying what you are afraid of or why you think you cannot handle a situation, then remind yourself: *There is an understanding self within me. This self is now wise and on top of every circumstance.*

Remind yourself of this very special self within you by naming the qualities and capabilities that you most need and desire at the moment. Clarify and name specifically the kind of nature and characteristics you want to be visible in your thoughts and emotions, speaking and living. Your whole being will respond. Practice going into the "closet" and shutting the door to any and all negative and limited considerations about yourself. See, instead, your oneness with the love and wisdom of God.

Whatever there is to understand—a child who throws tantrums, a sullen personality, a fearful encounter or circumstance, an emotional trauma, a loss of someone much loved, challenging pains of body or soul, or whatever else might arise—know that there is that self in you that understands.

The wonderfully helpful Unity textbook *Lessons in Truth* reminds us, "Sometimes you will be almost overcome by questions and doubts arising in your own mind when you are looking in vain for results. But you must with God's effort pass the place of doubt; and some day, in the fullness of God's time, while you are using the words of Truth, they will suddenly be illumined and become to you the living word within you—'the true light, even the light which lighteth every man, coming into the world' (Jn. 1:9 ASV) . . . This is spiritual understanding. This is a flash of the Most High within your consciousness."

The understanding self in you comprehends the value of nonresistance. This self understands that when needed and at the right time, helping hands will be extended from without, to lead you into the enfolding arms of the Shepherd. This beautiful, understanding self within you and within everyone awaits its opportunity to appear as you turn to its presence and acknowledge it.

This understanding self knows the right times for the "true light" to be unveiled to you as you are increasingly receptive through praise and thanksgiving. This self knows that you will never lose your way, never be separated from God, never miss sight of the goal of complete wholeness every child of God is meant to express.

Whether you sit in a classroom, drive your car, rest in your own place of privacy, or lie in a hospital room or clinic, you can find inner peace and healing assurance by remembering: *There is that self in me that understands. There is that in me that sees, knows, comprehends, and understands.*

A longtime friend recently experienced what he felt was the greatest challenge of his life. He remarked, "I thank God that I had a basis of understanding about myself—the presence of a self in me—to sustain me through a most frightening time. There were moments when I considered taking my life, but in those desperate moments, I remembered that the very presence and power of God lives within me and gives me the understanding I need to carry me through. Through this understanding, I developed a clearer image of myself along with a stronger conviction about my capabilities as God's creation and about the real purpose of my life."

A profound change in this man's attitude, demeanor, and appearance was evident to anyone. Yes, there is an understanding self within everyone. And this understanding self, this spirit of God in us, brings miracles of healing of every kind.

Jesus Christ, who understood all things from a divine point of view, could look without dismay into the worst of human appearances and perform needed miracles because of the understanding self in Him, united with the wisdom of the Father. He could see through everything that challenged the minds, souls, bodies, and lives of humans and bring about healing.

He understood God because He listened within and followed in spiritual boldness. He understood Himself because He acknowledged His divinity. He understood the workings of miracles because He approached each demand with His eyes and heart open to God and closed to all things called "impossible."

He understood the path He had chosen and was chosen for, and walked it all the way in spiritual comprehension, which came through consistent prayer and steady turning to God within. His understanding self carried Him through Gethsemane and broke through the tomb. He calls all children of God to follow Him in learning and understanding more about the innate God self that ever abides within us, awaiting recognition and release.

Yes, you, too, can understand the workings of your thoughts, feelings, body temple, and life. There is an understanding self in you.

Give Me This Day My Daily Bread

"Ask, and it will be given you; seek, and you will find; knock, and it will be opened to you. For every one who asks receives, and he who seeks finds, and to him who knocks it will be opened." — Mt. 7:7-8

"Our Father . . . . Give us this day our daily bread." — Mt. 6:9, 11

When you feel you have exhausted your prayer power and used all the faith at hand but still do not seem to be healed or fulfilled, do not be dismayed. There is more available. There is greater supply awaiting your acceptance. There is life more abundant at hand. There is a storehouse of peace, a fount of wisdom, ready and willing to outpour.

Let this added measure now come through and into the areas of your life that need it. With new spiritual boldness, affirm: *Father, give me this day, this moment, my "daily bread."* Accept in confidence that it is all right—in fact, it is imperative—that you claim your good as surely, as certainly, as specifically as the prodigal son who strayed from his inheritance.

Accept with confidence and assurance that it is all right to ask for and accept whatever nourishment of mind, soul, body, or life you need and desire. There is no limitation upon such a request, for *bread* is the terminology for substance that fulfills any kind of need in your life.

Jesus Christ knew this above and beyond the comprehension of anyone before or after Him. He counted on daily bread for every need and desire of His own heart's purposes and service to humankind. He knew where everything came from and did not hesitate to call for it, understanding that His relationship with God was secure and made stronger by His consistently turning to the Source, God.

Recently a Unity friend who had sought encouragement for his faith reported, "A friend of mine was starting a new electronics business. All kinds of trouble and setbacks (mostly people acting badly) had caused him anguish. I loaned him two of your books, and suggested that he try prayer. He did. Within the last month there has been a complete turnaround. Everything is proceeding well. His prayers were not answered just the way he expected, but in a better way. Rather than enduring the hopeless task of improving the new company, my friend is now with another company, with new management and a fine board of directors. Remarkable!"

The receiving of daily bread is not dependent just upon the Master's assured abundant desire to provide, but also upon your way of opening up to it. At times your nourishment may come through surprising channels — a new way, a willingness to keep on keeping on, a person, a place, or even a testing experience in your home or business. But the provision will come as you remember that God is the source and that He is the giver of every morsel of strength, peace, and material supply.

When a challenge is difficult for you to surmount and you feel you have reached the end of your rope, your courage, your faith, your understanding, or your trust, turn again to the prayer the Master has given to you and personalize it, directing your attention away from doubt and back to the words, "Give us this day our daily bread." State them clearly and with thankfulness: *Give me this day my daily bread, dear Father.*

Then remain receptive and expectant, knowing the supply will come through at the right time and in the right way. Know that your part in this cooperative action is not limited; it is acceptable to receive your good. It will come in the way you accept. This may be conscious acceptance, movement, action, or it may be unconscious inner receiving that comes quietly and unobtrusively to fulfill the need. Either way, the provision will come. The supply will be made visible. The good will be tangible. The solution and nourishment will appear.

Know also that you are, in reality, the God-created, fully attuned, spiritually equipped channel through which your good will flow. You are an appropriate vessel to receive the flow of the good. It will come in right order and harmony to bless you in every way, not so much as to be overpowering, but in perfect form, substance, and measure.

When your answers seem to be delayed or coming in the wrong fashion, remember that you can turn again to God. Ask for your daily bread of right receptivity, an open mind, heart, soul, and life.

From Father to Son, there is an orderly channeling of good. It may come in various ways, not because God is capricious, but simply because you are yet a growing, unfolding soul,

105

learning to accept your heritage, experiencing at times the variety of ways your soul is choosing to receive, even when you do not know it is happening. Do not be dismayed by obstacles or delays. Keep on in peace and thanksgiving, know you continually will be bettering your receptivity to God by consistent expectation from Him.

Affirm again and again: *Give me this day my daily bread, dear Father.* Then give thanks that you are receiving it moment by moment. As you are attentive and obedient to the Presence within, more and more of the kingdom's flow will come through and you will become accustomed to knowing God as an ever-providing presence of love and wisdom at hand.

At times the realization of this wonderful spiritual law of supply may almost seem to overwhelm you. At other times it may seem so slow that you think it will never come. No matter, this is part of your learning to accept your divine inheritance. It is partly the urging from the Holy Spirit to be faithful in looking always and only to God abiding within for your good. Practice trusting God for guidance in receiving. Consistently thank Jesus Christ for His helping hand and word and teaching. Trust yourself to be an open channel for receiving every good desire of your heart.

Speak the word daily in the same spiritual boldness that the Master did: *Give me this day my daily bread.* Give thanks to God, the giver of every good and perfect gift. The more often you ask and receive in acknowledgment of God as the loving source of everything good, the closer the union consciously becomes, until the awareness of its accompanying miracles flows through you as easily as it did through the Man of Galilee!

Do not hesitate to claim your nourishment and supply now. Remember, the supply is already available and waiting to be called for. There is only one place from which you ever receive good; it is from the kingdom of God within.

So, again, now, follow the One who knew and lived and proved the way of prayer given by Him to you: "Our Father, who art in heaven, hallowed be thy name. Thy kingdom come, Thy will be done, on earth as it is in heaven. Give us this day our daily bread" (Mt. 6:9-11).

Then give thanks that your good is already at hand.

There Is a Right Time for Everything

"For still the vision awaits its time . . . . If it seem slow, wait for it; it will surely come, it will not delay." —Hab. 2:3

There is a time to pray and a time to decree—a time to exercise your faith and authority as a child of God. There is a time to stop praying and to be still, to listen and to receive. There is a time to release all conscious effort and to just let go. There is a time to rest from struggle and to drop into the everlasting arms of the love of God.

There is a time to think about your challenges and to pursue your dreams and goals. There is a time to re-evaluate your life. There is a time to let yourself be renewed by Spirit and a time to go with the flow and trust all to God.

There is a time to know the truth with strong, affirmative words and direct action. There is a time to forget yourself by simply turning to help another in some way. There is a time to
108

relax, to enjoy being who you are, where you are.

There is a time for going through a wilderness and coming out with greater understanding of the power of Spirit. There is a time to help others through their difficult periods of life and a time to loose them and let them go. There is a time for planting seed ideas of wholeness, and a time to let them grow and bear fruit.

There is a time to learn, a time to share, a time to stand firm, and a time to give in to the good that will outpicture. There is a time to insist upon fairness and justice and a time to place every detail in God's wisdom and plan of unfoldment. There is a time to speak up and a time to be still and know that infinite Love is in control.

There is a time to read and to learn, and a time to let all words go, receiving quietly from an inner silence. There is a time to picture, a time to imagine the best, and a time to let a greater vision form and come through from on high. There is a time to question and to ask and a time to listen and to be taught and instructed. There is a time for unlearning as well as for learning anew.

There is a time for cleansing and for releasing the past. There is a time for starting again and for rebuilding faith, for letting all things be made new by the presence, power, and love of God. There is always the right time for birth and rebirth.

There is a time for moving along in a straight, smooth path of growing in understanding and a time for climbing rocks and mountains to test growing strengths. There is a time for walking and a time for resting beside the still waters. There is a time to get up again and place your hand in God's hand, moving forward toward your good. There is a time to let God lead you into experiences that you have not yet even thought of and a time to trust His leading as the very highest desire of a loving Father for a beloved offspring.

There is a time to rise up with conviction and to stand on your own rock of steady faith. There is a time to shout the truth and to revel in it, and a time to whisper it and to glory in His power within you and all.

For everything there is a time, and you will know the time. You will be guided in the right timing of everything in your life. You will know the right time to regroup, to meditate, to listen, and then to proceed to develop the indwelling spiritual capacities that are yours.

You will find the right time to do all things in order and to release all undue hurts without urgency. You will know the time to make haste

110

in peace and quietness, to be where you should be, and to quickly receive the blessings that await.

You will know there is even a right time for tears and weeping and then a time for drying the tears and taking action. You will know how to take time to let all undesirable emotion go and to let the infilling of God's love emerge fresh and new.

There is a time to scatter seeds of love, beauty, and Truth and a time to sweep together and garner blessings. You will find the right time to hear the voice of Spirit, to see the miracles of the Master, to ponder the glory of God.

There will be a right time for everything so that rebellion and frustration and resistance fall away, leaving you free to make the most of every moment, every experience. You will find that you have time for all that is to be done as well as time left to enjoy yourself.

Before Myrtle Fillmore, co-founder of Unity, entered her life's work and service, she had, as a schoolgirl, a beautiful dream about the source of life and wholeness. Her dream revealed a barren area of rock with but a trickling stream of water. She questioned the water's source. The answer came in a great outpouring of water over a high rocky ledge, so abundant that she watched in amazement, saying, later,

111

"This is one of my many dreams, the meaning of which was to be made plain afterwards." She later saw and understood more clearly the source of her life as "free flowing, more abundant Christ life." (*Myrtle Fillmore: Mother of Unity* by Thomas E. Witherspoon.)

For this wonderful woman, dedicated to finding the source of wholeness and sharing it with others, there was a right time for this vision and a right time later for totally overcoming a life-threatening illness. There was, for her, a time for serving humanity and a time for her moving quietly forward into her next life experience, even when others could not see her desire to do so. She knew and proved that there is a right time for everything.

Jesus was a divinely timed Master of life. He came to Bethlehem at the right time. He learned and matured, beginning His ministry at the right time. He walked His paths of service and healing and teaching at the right time, in the right places. He entered Jerusalem at the right time and remained in Gethsemane for the right time. Even the duration of His rock-sealed entombment was perfectly timed for the Resurrection to become a reality. For everything there is a right time.

As a growing and evolving person in this life, when I have fidgeted and rebelled against pressures, I have had to learn to wait upon God for His right time of revelation. When I experienced the deep loss of loved ones, there was a right time for letting go and for rebuilding my faith and trust in life more abundant. When I thought I hadn't enough strength to continue some project, I learned there was more energy within me than had appeared. When I became afraid of the issues of life or had need of healing, I knew it was the right time to launch into deeper awareness of God's love and to trust Him the more. I still learn and continue to be aware that there is a right time for everything, and that each moment of time holds a very special blessing.

For everything there is a right time, and there is that within you that will know when is the right time to go and do, to stop and listen, to seek and find, to let the spirit of God in you come fully into expression through your mind, heart, soul, and body. There is plenty of time for everything you desire to learn and do and be.

There is no haste in Spirit, only a divinely timed life of unfoldment of the child-of-God self within you, seeking to emerge through you. Relax all strain, efforts, and struggling. Know: *There is a right time for everything, for every good unfoldment in my life. Thank You, God.*

"He has made everything beautiful in its time . . . . Whatever God does endures for ever" (Eccles. 3:11, 14).

Give First to God

"Give, and it will be given to you; good measure, pressed down, shaken together, running over . . . . For the measure you give will be the measure you get back." —Lk. 6:38

Whatever your need, give your attention first to God. Give the best measure of your faith first to God, and be assured that increased measures of faith, peace, understanding, and healing will be measured to you in turn.

Give yourself, your attention, your thoughts to God now by speaking the words: *I trust and love God. I look to God first in everything.* Then take the steps needed to follow His guidance. Next, let go and let God's good work be done through you to bring healing and blessings.

When you think you have no more strength or courage left to give to your work, to your family, or to yourself, give an increased measure of attention to the reality of God dwelling in you. Know that there are depths of your own spiritual potential holding a supply of faith and conviction, calling for you to reach in and draw upon them and bring them forth into your con-

115

scious awareness, into the light of your own life.

Within you is a pearl of great price to be purchased simply by giving your thought wholly to God. Within you is the complete and infinite resource of all you need or desire. Consider this reality first. Turn to this Presence within first. Look to this indwelling power of God first. Give yourself to this first.

If you need peace at this moment and you wonder how it ever will be felt in the midst of your concerns and anxieties for yourself and those you love, settle down and relax by quietly turning within. Give yourself to God. Give Him your feelings, your doubts, your apprehensions regarding the future, your concerns of the present. Tell God, "Father, I come first to You. All this day I will listen first to You. I will give You the fullest measure of my attention. I will trust Your love to return to me pressed down and running over with the peace that passes all understanding. Thank You, God."

Each time a thought of concern enters your mind, quickly return to the thought, "Father, I come first to You. I give myself first to You. I accept the abundant measure of Your help and healing now." As you remember God first, your guidance will come. As you affirm God first, your assurance will increase. As you persist and

116

give thanks in acknowledging God first, your needs will be met in good measure and abundant supply.

Within you is the peace you dream about, the contentment your heart seeks, the strength, power, and ability you think others possess in greater degree. Within you now is the love you feel you have missed or lost, or never can have. Help is always ready and available for you to claim and accept when you come to God first.

If ever there was One who was not timid about turning first to God to supply His needs, it was the Son of God, Jesus of Nazareth. Oh, how clearly He asked, sought, prayed, talked, and gave of Himself totally to God. It is evident that He did not always immediately know the answers, but He gave His time to listening, His being to remaining quiet and responsive, His mind to receiving from the wisdom of God indwelling. He gave everything of Himself first to God, then to the multitudes' calls for help and healing. He gave as He learned and grew in stature, knowing that in giving Himself first to God, and then to the needs of humanity, God would work through Him to provide.

When He was called upon to come quickly to help those He dearly loved, Mary, Martha, and Lazarus, He again turned first to God, giving His attention to the source of all life and

117

healing. "He stayed two days longer in the place where he was" (Jn. 11:6). He gave time to the Father in inner quietness and responsive listening before saying, "Let us go" (Jn. 11:7), and walking to Judea to answer the needs of His friends. Only then was He ready to give outwardly the reassurance and comfort for which the situation and the people called.

Then His words and actions came from an inner realm of developed awareness that He had touched by giving Himself first to God's guidance. Because of His strong personal attachments to those involved, He wept and was troubled along with those who sorrowed over Lazarus' death. Yet in this very touching experience, Jesus' giving Himself first to God must have brought Him into a new dimension of power that He perhaps had not approached in His previous workings of miracles for so many.

In this particular instance, Jesus had given Himself to God for a long period of time in prayer and listening. He continued to give first to God in each successive step that He took. Only in this way could He have effectively put aside the moaning and groaning and weeping, and raised the loudest voice of all, knowing what it meant to give all of Himself first to God, in this greatest of all personal demands.

118

When an experience in your life is trying you to the utmost and you think you already have given all to the Father, do not hesitate to give again—even more of yourself in every way you know to His presence, His power, and His love. If you think you have exhausted the depths of your belief, remember the Master's earlier urging to His disciples who, having caught no fish, had hung up their empty nets to be washed and concluded their fishing efforts in discouragement for the day. His words, "Put out into the deep and let down your nets" (Lk. 5:4) rang out so clearly to them that they unhesitatingly returned to the same place that had been unproductive before in spite of their laboring to receive.

This time, however, they were acting with increased awareness that God was working with them in all they were doing. Now through the Master's urging, they were giving themselves to the spirit of success, to believing, first. They were returning to work in an awareness of God first. As a result, they found what had been awaiting them all the time—increased measure, overflowing, which broke the nets because of its weight.

During times when things are not going as well as I would like, I repeatedly have found a need just to stop everything for a while, to become like a little child—quiet, willing, and obedient in acknowledging the presence of God. I give myself first to God's presence and power, to His wisdom, love, and guidance, telling Him: "Yes, God. I am listening and trusting. I will follow Your directions first."

As you give first to God, you will receive abundantly from His infinite storehouse of peace, strength, and healing life. You will not always know how much of yourself you are or are not giving to God, so it is important to give consistently more of your time, attention, trust, and obedience. In this way the wellspring is tapped, and the unlimited treasures of the wholeness you seek are revealed and become tangible.

There is never a need to continue in despair, for God's help is at hand. Turning to God first will prove this reality!

As the day follows night, so giving yourself first to God produces more miracles of inner peace and outer blessings, greater awareness of your oneness with God and your spiritual potential. Give yourself first to God, and all the good heretofore delayed will follow.

Father, Thy Good Will Be Done

"If you . . . know how to give good
gifts to your children, how much more
will your Father who is in heaven give
good things to those who ask
him!"—Mt. 7:11

You need never be afraid of God's will, for
His will is always and only good. God wants
you to be healed. God wants you to be at
peace. God wants you to prosper and to be provided for in every way, in this life and always.

Whatever you are facing at this stage of your
life, take a moment to acknowledge, "Father, I
am willing. Thy good will be done!" As you let
go your own ideas about what needs to be done
and give yourself to the idea of obedience to
God's will, you will be amazed at the peace you
will begin to feel.

Let go right now, and quietly affirm: *Father, I
am willing. Thy good will be done.* Keep turning
your thoughts to the truth that God's will is
good in every way. There is nothing to be afraid
of.

Above all, Jesus Christ taught of the love of God for all His children. Jesus Christ brought this spiritual truth into practical words by saying, "What man of you, if his son asks him for bread, will give him a stone? Or if he asks for a fish, will give him a serpent? ... How much more will your Father who is in heaven give good things to those who ask him!" (Mt. 7:9-10, 11)

Cultivate an attitude of willingness by affirming: *Father, I am willing. Thy good will be done.* Cease all fearfulness that the will of God is anything but the highest and best for you. Know that His love knows and understands you far better than you can understand yourself at present.

Because of this love, God will provide the wisdom and motivation within you to place you upon the path of healing. God's will leads to the fulfillment of hopes and dreams you do not comprehend yet.

To become as willing as a child is one of the great blessings of the seeker of more abundant life. This is not a childish attitude, but a child-like, simple trust in the goodness of God. As God's child, you can trust the ways and the growing processes of your developing self to Him.

If you find yourself in a situation in which

you see no good occurring, no help available, no encouragement at hand, nothing to help you feel sure of yourself, remember to tell yourself again: *Father, I am willing. Thy good will be done.* This kind of acceptance will relax you immediately, release your human struggling and striving, and help you to realize that there is a Presence and Power working in this time, for and with you, and that it knows how to bring you into the healing and blessing you are seeking right here and now.

Jesus was motivated to enter the wilderness because He was willing to learn and to be obedient, to fast from all human doubt and disbelief for a period of time until He touched the reality of His indwelling power and capabilities. He was willing to trust the processes of His development as a Son of God at work within the wilderness experience.

Through His willingness and obedience to the Holy Spirit, Jesus Christ emerged from that period of learning with a realization that He had fulfilled the highest mission of anyone on earth. He gave Himself willingly to the workings of God within Him. There is no indication that Jesus Christ, at this time, fully understood what was going on; but there is evidence that He stood His ground in the highest and best way of obedience to the will of God.

123

Something good is always going on within you when you follow spiritual guidance to the best of your ability. You may not understand what God is doing within you during a time of challenge, but as surely as you need not dig into the ground to watch the unfolding seed develop into a plant or flower, you need not be concerned with how God's love brings answers to your prayers, your good, into expression. You need only to be obedient and willing to let it be done, to trust, as God's child, the healing processes of your Father.

The motivation you need to feel, the orderly steps you need to take, the supply of anything you need in mind or heart or body during the time of special growing and maturing will be provided. The environment will promote and nourish your best efforts to grow in spirit.

The Father's will for you and for all is good. It is, indeed, difficult to remember this when you face great challenges, when you cannot feel the faith you thought you possessed or the courage or peace you desire. But this is the time to remind yourself: *Father, I am willing. Thy good will be done.*

Release your urge to figure out the reasons; to probe how the challenge will be resolved, the questions answered or the difficulty healed. As a child, know that you can trust that God's

124

goodwill is at work in every moment of your existence. There is no place, no space, no time when God is not in action for your good.

The most difficult times in my personal growth experiences have been the days and nights and weeks and months when I have not felt the presence of God or known His assurance, when I have received no answers to my questions, no encouragement, no feeling of anything solved, nothing with which to bolster my wavering faith. In such times, I have found the prayer of willingness and obedience most helpful: *Father, I am willing. Thy good will be done.* This has been a powerfully stabilizing prayer and support through many "wilderness" periods. It has, in the right moments, brought the understanding and reassurance I longed for.

It is no wonder that the Master of obedience and willingness, Jesus Christ, incorporated the phrase "Thy will be done" within His prayer of prayers. He must have known that everyone needs not only to hear the words but to speak them and to comprehend them as reassurance that God's will is good. Everything Jesus Christ did proved God's good will: healing disease, raising the dead, feeding the hungry, and bringing peace and comfort to troubled hearts.

Later, when His prayer in Gethsemane again mentioned the Father's will and He prayed,

"My Father, if this cannot pass unless I drink it, thy will be done" (Mt. 26:42), His willingness and obedience had reached another point of supreme testing in order to fulfill His purpose in this life. This testing did not indicate that the Father's plan was less than the highest and best. It indicated that there was a powerful demand upon this Son of God to rise up to His highest potential as a Way-Shower for all humankind. It indicated that He had the strength and power to do so and that the supply of life would be equal to the demand of that experience.

Whatever the demand made upon you, the supply is forthcoming. Just as surely as the Resurrection resulted from the Master's willingness to rise to His full potential as the manifest Son of God so that all might see what they individually are in reality, so you can, through this little prayer, "Thy will be done," find yourself lifted to your divine potential as the image and likeness of God.

The most freeing, life-giving, resurrecting prayer ever prayed, voiced by Jesus of Nazareth, was, "Thy will be done." Here He set the supreme example of trust in God.

Yes, you have full right to pray in faith the ultimate prayer, "Thy will be done," and thus experience the peace that passes all understanding.

Be Not Anxious

"Little children . . . I am with you."
—Jn. 13:33
"Let not your hearts be troubled . . . .
Where I am you may be also."
—Jn. 14:1, 3

If you are afraid of anything at all, worried about circumstances in your life or about someone dear to you, come now into the great love of the Father and rest a while from all concern. Tell yourself softly, calling yourself by name, "Be not anxious. Let not your heart be troubled."

As the very beloved and precious child of God, you were never intended to be anxious about yourself, or another, or anything. This is true, not because your life is perfect or because you do not care for others or feel deeply at times of challenge, but because there is a resilient spirit of God within you ready to lift you up and hold you securely, relieving your every burden.

Be not anxious. There is nothing to fear. You are an invulnerable spiritual offspring of the Most High. You have within you the might of the Holy Spirit, the wisdom of the Father, and

127

the capabilities of a child of God.

Be not anxious. You need not jump from this moment into tomorrow or next week or next month or next year trying to solve all that you think may test or burden you. You live in this moment only, with the reassurance that each day you will be given the all-sufficiency to fulfill your every need. You now can choose to live in a "day-tight" compartment of faith, reminding yourself, "Be not anxious. Let not your heart be troubled."

Be not anxious. Because you have been created in the image of the Father, you can choose to react positively to anything appearing unpleasant or threatening. You have within yourself a powerful rebounding spirit of God, an inner fortification of continuous peace, a garrison of order and wisdom to protect and support you and to show you how to accept God's guidance and deliverance moment by moment and how to turn all things to good.

Be not anxious. Within you is a spiritual remembrance of an inherited conviction of your oneness with God. God has made you in His likeness of greatness and placed the complete fullness of every strength within the depths of your soul.

Be not anxious. There is a wise and loving unfolding pattern for your learning and growing in
128

this lifetime and forever. You need not know now how all this will come about. You can simply praise and give thanks for your spiritual heritage as the Father's child. You will find healing and blessing by quietly remembering that God already has given "his angels charge of you to guard you in all your ways" (Ps. 91:11). You always will have the help of the right ideas, the right people, the right happenings to keep you on the path of ever-increasing wholeness and well-being.

Be not anxious. Let not your heart be troubled about what you shall eat or wear or have or be or do. Rather, know that all these things will be ordered aright by infinite love and wisdom, for "your heavenly Father knows that you need them all" (Mt. 6:32). As you release undue worry about them, they are released into their right form, function, and purpose and for the benefit of your mind and body and life.

Because Jesus fed the multitudes, you know He accepted healthful food as part of the blessing of life and its sustaining nourishment. Because He produced the tangible substance of money, you know He did not resist taking care of material needs in a humanly practical way. Because He was spoken of as wearing a seamless garment, you know He did not reject presenting an appearance of well-being in keeping

129

with the times and customs.

When He spoke of giving no thought to life's daily needs, He did not demean sound judgment and considerate care for human needs. He evidently was aware of the importance of a strong, positive attitude toward everything in daily life and rendered the appropriate degree of importance to each, always giving, however, undue concern over details to the Father.

Be not anxious does not mean ignoring a need or a problem. It means knowing that personal anxiety has no place in a mind or heart that can choose, instead, to remember and trust God. Whatever the needs might be for your life, your body, your home, your work, or your dear ones, you need not let your heart be troubled. At any moment when you find yourself becoming agitated, unsure, or upset, you can choose to remember your spiritual identity as a child of God. You can tell yourself quietly, "Be not anxious." In this way, you begin to move instantly in the direction of your inherited wholeness of peace, order, and well-being.

Thought by chosen thought, you can give yourself and all into the healing, peace-restoring, life-producing idea: *Be not anxious. Let not your heart be troubled.* As often as needed, you can repeat the words, relaxing again and again in mind and body and emotion, finding that there is a response within you, a new quietness flowing through you. You will find within yourself an established remembrance of trust and knowing that always has been there. It is the steady, solid foundation that is ready to support and uphold you always.

Upon this rock of spiritual remembrance you can build your deepening awareness of faith, your awakening thoughts of your true identity as an offspring of God, your spiritual dwelling place of understanding of oneness with God. Prayer by prayer, accepting this already established, remembered center of peace and calm within you, you will find fortification of your belief in yourself, in God's presence and power, and in your life's pattern of soul-unfoldment.

Building decree by decree, idea upon idea, perception by perception, and action by action upon the reality of your wholeness as a child of God, you will become gradually more aware of the power of the God dwelling within and less and less troubled about anything.

When Peter revealed his recognition of Jesus' Son of God identity, Jesus spoke the words, "On this rock [His reality as a Son of God recognized and accepted] I will build my church" (Mt. 16:18). Because He already had called attention to the fact that His words were spirit, you can be sure that He was speaking of His "church" not as an outer structure or worldly organization but as an inner awareness, as an inner habitation and dwelling place wherein God-ideas, whole ideas, and healing perceptions, thoughts, and feelings of the goodness and greatness of the Father would dwell and flourish.

As you remember and accept this reality, you begin to activate that awareness consciously, to permit it to be quickened and strengthened. This is the structure of your own growing concepts and comprehension of your oneness with God.

Be not anxious. The process of awakening may seem very slow at times, I know, and you may not be aware of the growing, of the rebuilding of your acceptance of the inherent faith and powers of healing and loving, hearing and seeing, of the presence of God within yourself and others. But the activity is quickened and recharged with every prayer you pray, every moment you choose to turn from anxiety to trusting and believing in the living, breathing, healing Christ as Peter did when he called out in sudden recognition, "You are the Christ, the Son of the living God" (Mt. 16:16).

Carry this awakened faith faculty, as seen here in Peter, into times of prayer, and call on

132

that same recognition of the inmost self of you. You are the child of the living God, with every inherited potential of the Son of God. As a building is built brick by brick, so your inner habitation of recognized wholeness and healing and peace and life is built thought by thought, word by word, action by action, day by day.

Be not anxious. The builder and maker of your every growing experience of life is always God, the one giver of every gift. You are God's co-creator and co-worker in every accomplishment. Jesus assures you that He came so that your joy may be made full in this process. It is intended to be a joy, for when you see that each step is gain, your anxieties and concerns are transformed into thankfulness and praise.

Be not anxious. Let not your heart be troubled. In my daily seeking and searching for inner equanimity, peace, and release of concerns, I find that surfacing irritability, critical feelings, and impatience with myself or others arise frequently from an accumulation of anxieties that have hidden themselves in obscure recesses of thought and feeling. When these outer signs show themselves, I have been healed and restored by the thought: *Be not anxious. Let not your heart be troubled.* Remembering and repeating these words has been effective in bringing peace and healing for myself and others.

Be not anxious. Peter's burst of recognition of Jesus as "Christ, the Son of the living God" shows you that there can be a holy recognition, a divine remembrance in you, too, in any challenging circumstance. You recall that before this moment, Peter was, at times, unfaithful, unreliable, and even extremely fearful in acknowledging the identity of the Master. Take heart from this. No matter how lacking you feel you are in substantial faithfulness toward God, an inner remembrance of your reality always is waiting at the door of your thought to spring forth into an instantaneous acceptance of the Christ spirit within Jesus and within yourself as His joint heir.

Be Thou Made Whole

"And as many as touched it [His garment] were made well." — Mt. 14:36

"For with God nothing will be impossible." — Lk. 1:37

There is a flowing life stream of healing that ever invites you to step into its currents and be made whole. As you sit quietly and read those words, thinking about healing for yourself or for another, know, accept, and give thanks that the life stream of healing flows not only all about you but also within every cell and atom of your body temple now. In your mind's eye, see yourself stepping into the current and being made whole.

Each idea of healing presented to you at any moment helps you to walk into a newly quickened awareness that healing is here and is meant to be received. Give your thoughts, feelings, and mental imaginings to the flow of healing life. Invite it consistently, insistently, even boldly, into this experience of your life, whatever challenge may appear.

See yourself moving step by step into wholeness in that area of your being where you need to see it made visible. Tell yourself: *I step into the current, and I am made whole.*

This life stream of healing was augmented with a marvelous wave of new power, a sweep of fresh, pure substance of wholeness and well-being for all humankind with the birth of Jesus in Bethlehem. All the heavens sang for joy because of His arrival with the message of healing. The earth heralded healing with expectation and joy. The quiet shepherds watched with praise and glory to God. All creation opened its arms to receive the Prince of Peace bringing the message of healing of everything for humanity and the universe.

The life stream of healing swelled in increasing waves of activity as the boy grew and learned, as He listened and taught, and as every manner of disease began to give way to His words and works of spirit and life. His undeniable love for humankind and His overwhelming love for God cut through the fog of disbelief and lifted the inner eyes of His followers to the healing presence of God.

His voice, "like the sound of many waters" (Rev. 1:15) flowing, washed away fears. His hands carried the touch of miracle-working gentleness and strength. His look of compassion wiped away old hurts and pains and deformities of soul, making whole the multitudes. Nothing was impossible to the Man of Galilee, and nothing was incurable.

This "Savior," "Master," "Son of God" tells you today that He came to bring you the life, joy, peace, and provision you are meant to experience in this life on earth. He tells you through His words and His works that healing is for everyone without exception. And He sets forth clearly and simply the ways and means through which it is to be accomplished and realized.

He speaks of the thoughts of the mind and how to direct them wisely, to place them under the guidance of Spirit. He tells you of the importance and power of your words and how to use them with authority. He talks about the necessity of denying negative appearances of any kind and about the value of affirmatively declaring the goodness of the one true Presence and Power—God. He repeatedly reminds you that by your thoughts, words, and actions your healing is justified!

He tells you that any unhealthy appearances within your world are not worthy of your time or energy, that an attitude of resistance is to be replaced by positive response to His ways and truth and life, so that the full tide of healing may sweep through your being and restore wholeness to every part of you.

He revealed that there are many ways of healing and that you have choices of acceptance. You will know what is best for you. Whether you seek wholeness in one way or in another, through one method or through another, His love opens up the realization that the Father will move into any channel or opening and flood it with His life stream of well-being.

Jesus Christ emphatically urged your willingness to accept the cleansing of the inner, hidden realms of your mind and heart so that the causes of difficulty could be dissolved. This urging was, in His way of working, accomplished without even an inkling of awareness on the part of many of the recipients.

You can, at this moment, find freedom from any old belief that there is only one way of healing. There are infinite galaxies of healing ways, as many methods and channels as there are unlimited numbers of stars in the heavens. You have but to open your heart to accept the reality that healing is God's intent and purpose for you, His beloved offspring and heir.

God never responds with "no" to your desire for healing. Healing is an inevitable heritage that can become visible for anyone. No matter what the disease or difficulty, the message of Jesus Christ is healing.

If your healing does not appear to be soon enough, strong enough, complete enough, be assured another step is before you. You can come into the present moment with the powerful conviction: *I step into the current and I am made whole.*

Even though it has been thousands of years since His physical appearance upon the earth, His healing breath of life fills this planet still. His presence is here as the spirit and life you need within your mind and body now. The currents of His peace and strength and wholeness and well-being flow unceasingly all about you, within you. Step into this current and be thou made whole.

Perhaps you feel that your steps are so small and hesitant you will never reach your good. Take them anyway. You may fear stumbling and falling again; step forward anyway. Listen to His words again. Think of His works. Consider His life. Keep your eyes on His presence, your ears open to His guidance. Know: *This is His message to me—to step forward into the current and be made whole.*

His love is telling you, "Accept my healing presence over and above every doubt and fear. I have come for your blessing, and I remain here to bring you new life. I am here now to guide you into the very best channels of wholeness for your entire being. So listen, follow, and receive. My current of life flows unceasingly. Step into this current and be thou made whole."

Healing is inevitable. No matter what you have been told about your limitations, no matter what your own human reasoning tries to convey, your healing is possible. The Father intends healing for His children. God not only is the healing power within you, He also is you in the process of life expression, wholeness, love, peace, and all else that is good and desirable. Step into this current of life and you will be made whole.

When the woman diseased "for twelve years" pushed her way to the Master's side, whispering to herself, "If I only touch his garment, I shall be made well" (Mt. 9:21), she was showing all humanity that every struggling step was worth the effort. She was the example of every seeking soul walking step by step into closer awareness of total healing. She was the awakening belief that healing is possible, healing is personal, healing is God's will, and healing is attainable. As a result, she was instantly made well.

Healing is to be known and experienced not only within the body temple but also within every facet of life. Just as Jesus calmed the wind and the waves, we are the vehicles for the calming of every disturbed element within this precious universe.

God's will for healing includes peace among nations and peace in all relationships. The beginning for such peace and order and harmony lives within each individual.

The more of the Christ-healing concepts you receive and permit to motivate you, the more their reality, presence, and power will become visible in and through you. Healing is your purpose in life right where you are. Healing is the will of God for everyone everywhere. Let this current of His life stream now have new and unrestricted flow through you. Step into the current and be thou made whole.

Eyes that have not seen will see. Ears that have not heard will hear. Hearts that have been troubled will be made calm and serene. Limbs that have not functioned will be strengthened and restored to flexibility and freedom. Organs and muscles and nerves and cells that have been cramped and tight and restricted will open and be at ease. All this and more is God's will for His offspring. This is the message of His love, given through His manifest and visible Son.

He is with you all the way, encouraging you, motivating you again and again to take another step, and yet another, until you are caught up in the true light, the awareness of your indwelling wholeness as a child of the living God.

His life stream is flowing for you now. Its cleansing waves roll, to restore you now. Step into the current of His healing power and be thou made whole!

Printed U.S.A.

26-1776-7.5M-12-89